Language and Literacy Series

Dorothy S. Strickland, Celia Genishi,
and Donna Alvermann SERIES EDITORS

ADVISORY BOARD: Richard Allington, Donna Alvermann,
Kathryn Au, Bernice Cullinan, Colette Daiute, Anne Haas Dyson,
Carole Edelsky, Janet Emig, Shirley Brice Heath, Connie Juel,
Susan Lytle, Timothy Shanahan

Volumes in the NCRLL Set:
Approaches to Language and Literacy Research
JoBeth Allen and Donna Alvermann, SERIES EDITORS

On Formative and Design Experiments:
Approaches to Language and Literacy Research
David Reinking and Barbara Bradley

On the Case:
Approaches to Language and Literacy Research
Anne Haas Dyson and Celia Genishi

On Qualitative Inquiry:
Approaches to Language and Literacy Research
George Kamberelis and Greg Dimitriadis

D1016037

ON FORMATIVE AND DESIGN EXPERIMENTS

Approaches to Language and Literacy Research

(AN NCRLL VOLUME)

David Reinking
Barbara A. Bradley

Teachers College, Columbia University
New York and London

National Conference on
Research in Language and Literacy

Published by Teachers College Press, 1234 Amsterdam Avenue, New York, NY 10027

Published in association with the National Conference on Research in Language and Literacy (NCRLL). For more information about NCRLL, see *www. nyu.edu/education/teachlearn/research/ncrll*

Library of Congress Cataloging-in-Publication Data
On formative and design experiments : approaches to language and literacy research / David Reinking and Barbara A. Bradley.
     p. cm. — (Language and literacy series)
    Includes bibliographical references and index.
    ISBN 978-0-8077-4841-1 (pbk. : alk. paper)
    ISBN 978-0-8077-4842-8 (cloth : alk. paper)
     1. Reading—Research. 2. Language and languages—Research. I. Reinking, David. II. Bradley, Barbara A.
    LB1050.6.O5 2008
    428.407′2—dc22   2007030563

ISBN 978–0-8077–4841–1 (paper)
ISBN 978–0-8077–4842–8 (cloth)

Printed on acid-free paper
Manufactured in the United States of America

15 14 13 12 11 10 09 08   8 7 6 5 4 3 2 1

Contents

From the NCRLL Editors

Are you in search of an approach to studying literacy interventions in classrooms that is a collaboration between teachers and university researchers? Do you prefer an approach to classroom research that takes into account the day-to-day variations in students' learning and teachers' instructional decision making? Would it be helpful if such an approach had built-in mechanisms for fine tuning your research design as a result of changes in a school's demographic make-up, curricular goals, or staff turnover? If you answered yes to one or more of these questions, chances are this book—*On Formative and Design Experiments*, by David Reinking and Barbara Bradley—will be well worth the time you spend reading it.

The third volume in a collection of books that offer definitive information and guidance in using different research approaches in the field of language and literacy education, *On Formative and Design Experiments* follows in the tradition of the two earlier volumes in the collection: *On Qualitative Inquiry*, by George Kamberelis and Greg Dimitriadis, and *On the Case*, by Anne Haas Dyson and Celia Genishi. Future volumes in this collection, sponsored by the National Conference on Research in Language and Literacy (NCRLL) and published by Teachers College Press, will deal with the topics of ethnography (authored by Shirley Brice Heath and Brian Street), critically conscious research (authored by Arlette Willis and colleagues), classroom discourse (authored by David Bloome and colleagues), teacher inquiry (authored by Marty Rutherford and colleagues), narrative inquiry (authored by David Schaafsma and Ruth Vinz), mixed methods (authored by Robert Calfee and Melanie Sperling), and quantitative research methods (authored by P. David Pearson and Barbara Taylor).

As with other volumes in the NCRLL collection, *On Formative and Design Experiments* presents this approach's theoretical assumptions, its issues and tensions (including different interpretations, applications, methods), possible research questions that might be addressed, and numerous exemplars of published research within this emerging methodology. The authors, who are influential scholars in the area of formative experiments in literacy education, draw on their first-hand experiences in using this relatively new approach to conducting classroom research.

On Formative and Design Experiments offers a fresh approach to the current stalemate in large funded research efforts. At a time when federally funded initiatives are seeking to bring research studies on literacy interventions to scale, Reinking and Bradley cogently argue for an approach that is a building block to a scaled-up design. Established scholars and doctoral students who are interested in broadening their repertoire of research methods, as well as editors and reviewers who may be asked to pass judgment on the rigor of research reports using this approach, will find *On Formative and Design Experiments* to be a useful book.

Acknowledgments

We gratefully acknowledge the assistance and support of several individuals and agencies in the creation of this book. Foremost, we are grateful for the collegial support and guidance that we received from Donna Alvermann and JoBeth Allen, the NCRLL series editors. Their insights, sensitively communicated, were invaluable in helping us enhance the readability and utility of this book for its intended audience. We also appreciate their willingness to include this relatively new approach among the more mainstream approaches in the series. Similarly, we are grateful for the honest feedback provided by Tom Reeves, Robert Calfee, and Lee Williams, who reviewed an early draft of the manuscript. Their comments encouraged us to consider several topics more deeply and to refine and clarify many of the concepts, ideas, and issues we discussed. Nonetheless, readers should not assume that they have endorsed the final product, nor should they be held accountable for any omissions or errors.

We wish to thank the staff at Teachers College Press, who supported this book and who worked diligently to refine and consolidate our efforts. Our work on the book began under the able direction of Carol Collins, our acquisitions editor. When Carol left the Press in March of 2007, Meg Lemke, her successor, capably took over the reins. Assisting Meg and working with us on the final stages of production and publication of the book were Adee Braun, Tamar Elster, and Shannon Waite. They all do important work that is essential for bringing a project such as this one to fruition, and they carried out their work in a friendly and professional manner.

We also wish to acknowledge the funding agencies that have supported our research. That support has allowed us to gain first-hand experience in conducting formative experiments, to explore the conceptual boundaries of that approach, and to clarify our thinking about it on a scale that would not have been possible without funding. We are particularly grateful for the generous support provided by the former Office of Educational Research and Instruction and currently the Institute of Education Sciences in the United States Department of Education. Nonetheless, it is important to note that none of the agencies supporting our work necessarily endorse the perspectives, findings, or conclusions presented in this book. Our appreciation of the support provided by these agencies extends further to the administrators, teachers, and students who have graciously allowed us to conduct research in their schools and classrooms and who have typically collaborated closely with us.

Finally, we wish to thank our families and close colleagues for their support, mainly through their unselfish patience and understanding in allowing us to work long hours on this project. They often sacrificed their needs and excused us from obligations to accommodate the reading, contemplating, discussing, and writing that were necessary to complete this project. We hope that our efforts are worthy of their support, for which we are truly grateful.

Introduction

Our task in this book is, of necessity, somewhat different from that of the authors of the other books in this series. Compared to the other methodologies and approaches presented in this series, formative and design experiments represent a new, emerging way to conceptualize and conduct research. Formative and design experiments do not have a long tradition of widespread use inside or outside the community of literacy researchers. They are rarely used, if at all, among researchers in disciplines unrelated to education, although that is because this approach originated within and, we would argue, is especially suited to the field of education. Further, there is not always agreement about the essence of this new approach, nor is there stability in its terminology; currently there are no book-length, consensual expositions of its practice.

Given that state of affairs, one might reasonably ask why this approach was included at all among the more established and more widely used methodologies in this series. Primarily, it is because formative and design experiments have attracted a growing interest among education researchers with diverse orientations and interests. That interest is grounded fundamentally in a quest among many researchers to find methods uniquely suited to the ultimate goals of education research, particularly to reducing the gap between research and practice. Formative and design experiments, or what has been referred to more generally as *design research,* is poised to advance that perennial quest and to enter the mainstream of methodologies employed by educational researchers.

For example, three respected research journals have devoted themed issues to this approach to research: *Educational Researcher* (2003, Vol. 32, No. 1), *Educational Psychologist* (2004, Vol. 39, No. 4), and *The Journal of the Learning Sciences* (2004, Vol. 13, No. 1).

In addition, an edited book titled *Educational Design Research* (van den Akker, Gravemeijer, McKenney, & Nieveen, 2006) has extended thinking about the conceptual basis of this new approach and gives testimony to the international attention it has received. Likewise, a chapter on design experiments appears in the *Handbook of Complementary Methods in Education Research,* sponsored by the American Educational Research Association (Schoenfeld, 2006). Readers are also referred to a website maintained by the Design-Based Research Collective: http://www.designbasedresearch.org.

Another reason is that this approach has firm roots in literacy research. Ann Brown (1992), most known for her laboratory approach to conducting conventional experiments related to the metacognitive aspects of reading comprehension, is widely recognized as having first articulated the rationale for and the practice of this approach. She gravitated toward design experiments as she grappled with the difficulties inherent in translating and implementing the results of her tightly controlled laboratory experiments into the messy, less controlled world of classrooms. In addition, the early work of Luis Moll (e.g., Moll & Diaz, 1987), aimed at understanding and improving the literacy of Latino students, embraced from the outset an orientation to research quite similar to formative and design experiments, although he did not use that terminology.

The fact that researchers as diverse in their orientations as Ann Brown and Luis Moll might find common ground within their research agendas points to another reason that formative and design experiments merit inclusion in this series. This approach to research promises to transcend many of the methodological and epistemological differences that divide the literacy research community. It does so by uniting two fundamental urges that motivate many educational researchers: to gain deep theoretical understandings of teaching and learning and to use those understandings to make education more effective and enriching.

Formative and design experiments bring researchers into classrooms in a way that naturally fosters collaborative relationships with teachers (and with each other, often in interdisciplinary design teams), thus avoiding to some extent the issues of power, privilege, and authenticity that have been noted as problematic when researchers do their work in classrooms. Formative and design experiments do not eliminate these issues, and in some circumstances may even exacerbate them, but they provide a unique opportunity for confronting and resolving potential tensions between the roles of researchers and teachers as they collaborate to achieve common goals.

Formative and design experiments seem to resonate particularly well with classroom teachers, at least once they shed their conventional notions about what educational research is and what education researchers do. Ideally, they come to discover that this approach is simply a more systematic, intense, and data-driven way of doing what they do every day: setting pedagogical goals, making instructional moves to accomplish those goals, determining what works or doesn't work in helping or hindering the achievement of those goals, making appropriate adjustments, and assessing and reflecting on what has been accomplished. In short, formative and design experiments not only more naturally bridge the often-lamented gap between research and practice; they exist squarely in the interface between them.

Our own paths to embracing this approach reflect the reasons that other researchers have found it attractive and useful. In the case of the elder, more experienced first author, who came of age as a literacy researcher when scientific experiments were de rigueur, it was a failed attempt to conduct a tightly controlled experiment to study the effects of a classroom intervention (see Reinking & Pickle, 1993). A poignant moment in that failed effort came during a post mortem debriefing when there was a pregnant pause after one of the researchers referred to a teacher as a *nuisance variable.* For the second author, it was a gradual realization that a formative experiment not only allowed her to address the questions she wished to pursue in her dissertation research, but also that this approach was well matched to the instincts and sensitivities she had acquired as a preschool special education teacher as well as her commitment to developing young children's literacy and improving instruction toward that end.

Finally, we state two caveats. First, because this book is about an emerging approach to research, it does not represent a definitive and final statement about what formative and design experiments are or how they should be conceptualized and conducted. Nonetheless, we hope that it extends the dialogue about and the use of this promising approach, and we hope that it will be a useful guide to those who wish to understand and use it.

The second caveat is the risk that our own experiences in using this approach may overly influence our conceptualization and interpretation of it. That risk was clear as we read the comments and perspectives of the reviewers who read an earlier draft. We wish to thank those reviewers for their constructive suggestions and comments. Nonetheless, even after revision, many of our original perspectives remain.

Finally, we welcome comments from readers, who are invited to contact us through e-mail. We look forward to a continued discussion of this evolving approach.

—David Reinking, reinkin@clemson.edu
—Barbara A. Bradley, barbarab@ku.edu

CHAPTER 1

What Are Formative and Design Experiments?

Understanding the essence of formative and design experiments and the methodological orientation they represent has much to do with how research relates to instructional practice. Thus, to answer the overarching question of this chapter, we begin with a consideration of that relation. As a preface to subsequent sections where we more specifically characterize the dimensions of formative and design experiments, we first step back to consider how research and practice have been related beyond the boundaries of education and literacy research. We start with a few examples illustrating the legitimacy of and the need for approaches to research aimed at addressing practical problems, developing workable solutions, and accomplishing valued goals. These examples illustrate that such approaches are common in other fields of research, although largely absent in education. We then compare and contrast how a few imaginary doctoral students' selection of a dissertation topic might be influenced by their views of methodology, including one student who chooses to conduct a formative or design experiment. Our intent is to highlight some of the fundamental ideas underlying the rationale for formative and design experiments and to preview some of the dominant themes of this approach.

The first set of examples is from Stokes (1997), who argued that creating a dichotomy between basic and applied research is relatively recent in the history of science. He thought that dichotomy to be unnatural and inconsistent with the history of scientific inquiry. Historically, he argued, science, including theory development, has often advanced in the pursuit of solving real problems or bringing about desirable ends. Basic, purely theoretical research (i.e., research focused on testing theory without a concern for its practical utility) is not typically the engine that drives the advancement of knowledge and its application. Instead, theory often follows or emerges concomitantly with invention and discovery. The central thesis of his argument is captured in Figure 1.1, showing four quadrants of possible relations between fundamental understanding on one hand and consideration of use on the other. Each quadrant provides a quintessential example of a researcher who worked in that quadrant.

Consistent with Stokes's argument, formative and design experiments, conceptually and methodologically, fall decidedly and purposefully on the right side of Figure 1.1. In our view, depending on a particular researcher's methodological and disciplinary grounding, formative and design experiments oscillate between the upper-right and lower-right quadrants. That is, they may lean toward the derivation of theoretical understandings in the context of addressing a practical problem, such as Pasteur's development of theories about microorganisms in the context of his efforts to preserve food. Or they may lean toward the more engineering perspective represented by Edison, who focused primarily on developing a useful product, but who nonetheless drew on basic scientific understandings of electricity and whose work furthered those understandings as a by-product of his creative invention. Education researchers conducting a formative or design experiment likewise attempt to bring about positive change in education environments through creative, innovative, instructional interventions grounded in theory and guided by systematic data collection and analysis. They use available theoretical understandings, but they are more interested in testing those theories in the real world of teaching and learning in classrooms, and they expect to refine and to modify those theories in the course of their work.

Figure 1.1. Quadrant Model of Scientific Research

| | | Consideration of Use? | |
		No	Yes
Quest for Fundamental Understanding?	Yes	Pure basic research: Niels Bohr	Use-inspired basic research: Louis Pasteur
	No		Pure applied research: Thomas Edison

Source: Stokes, D. E. (1997).

We wish to note that although the lower-left quadrant lacks an example, it is not necessarily an empty cell. In fact, some researchers invested in the rationale for formative and design experiments would argue that too much education research exists in that quadrant. For example, horserace-like studies pitting one instructional intervention against another using statistical comparisons of relatively narrow measures contribute little to understanding or to use (e.g., see Reeves, Herrington, & Oliver, 2005). Many researchers who gravitate toward formative and design experiments see the need for an approach to research that provides richer, more meaningful information that contributes directly to practitioners' need not only to find workable instructional options but also to provide specific guidance about how to implement instructional interventions given the diverse variation in classrooms.

Another example is the Wright brothers' efforts to develop a flying machine. Like Edison, their work was aimed at developing a working product for a specific purpose. The basic theory that explains lift had existed since Daniel Bernoulli in the mid-18th century, but it had not been applied successfully to human flight. The Wright brothers' genius, however, was to create three-axis control that allowed predictable maneuverability. As Schoenfeld (2006) pointed out, the application of basic theory to a practical problem led in this instance to an entirely new set of theories that created the field of aerodynamics. As he stated, "There are times when one has to create something to explore its properties" (p. 193), and by extension a new domain of theories. For example, the rudimentary principles of controlling flight pioneered by the Wright brothers were extended eventually to maintaining control in a wide range of atmospheric conditions. And the research methodologies that allowed for the refinement of those principles included both the controlled conditions of the wind tunnel and the less controlled conditions explored by test pilots.

From the perspective of researchers interested in formative and design experiments, the work of literacy researchers who do conventional, highly controlled experiments is analogous to conducting research in a wind tunnel. Likewise, researchers who use more naturalistic methods are typically analogous to meteorologists who describe patterns of atmospheric conditions that airplanes must fly in. But such information is only indirectly useful to designing a real aircraft. Nonetheless, in the history of education and literacy research, there is no category of research analogous to the work of designers, engineers, and test pilots whose coordinated efforts are aimed directly at getting an airplane to fly and to perform for specific purposes under a variety of conditions. For example, literacy researchers rarely, if ever, consider defining thresholds of failure for a promising instructional activity (see Sloane & Gorard, 2003; Wagner, 1993). Yet setting those thresholds is fundamental to designing an airplane, and addressing that information often leads to new understandings and in turn to new modes and approaches to flight.

Formative and design experiments represent an approach to research that fits the latter analogy, because they are aimed at discovering workable instruction and relevant theory in the real world. And although this approach doesn't try to create failure, it is not afraid of it either, because failures and setbacks in trying to create instruction aimed at accomplishing a pedagogical goal are at least as important for understanding and effective implementation as are successes. As Walker (2006) stated, "Every form of practice degrades under severe conditions. We need [instructional] designs that degrade gracefully rather than catastrophically" (p. 13). Like the Wright brothers, researchers who use formative and design experiments draw on basic theory, but that theory must not only be elegantly appealing on an intellectually abstract level, it must do real work in creating and explaining instruction (Cobb et al., 2003a). In addition, researchers who use this approach to research expect to find new theoretical insights that transform or transcend the basic theory, perhaps even leading to new theoretical domains grounded in practice.

The underlying metaphor of research in this vein is engineering. Traditionally and historically, in the field of education in general and literacy in particular, the task of engineering workable instruction has been left mostly to practitioners, not researchers. That is, practitioners have been left to their own devices to determine how research might be applied to their practice. Or, when researchers attempt to translate their work into practice, that activity is viewed, at best, as an extension, not as an integral part, of their research. For example, doctoral students are often advised to seek publication of their dissertation in a research journal, such as *Reading Research Quarterly,* and then to write a separate piece for practitioners translating the implications of their research for publication in a practitioner outlet, such as *The Reading Teacher.*

On the contrary, formative and design experiments intimately merge research and practice, producing findings more transparent and useful to practitioners. Put another way, before formative and design experiments, education research had nothing equivalent to engineering science as a testing ground for ideas and for the application and development of theory within a systematic attempt to accomplish specific ends in real classrooms. Sloane and Gorard (2003) have even raised the question of whether education research should more appropriately exist within the realm of engineering science rather than social science. Going even further, Reeves (2006) argued that such an orientation is the only socially responsible approach to research in education.

A final example comes from what is called precision farming. Precision farming demonstrates how using precise local data produces higher yields as well as new understandings about complex interactions among many diverse variables. Normal farming makes use of much scientific theory and research that lead to recommendations about the most appropriate seed, fertilizer, and water given a particular climate, soil, and so forth. That information is typically generated and disseminated by governmental agencies and private companies, typically as broad generalizations for, at best, a particular region, although it is sometimes supplemented by a few randomized soil samples taken from a particular farm.

Precision farming allows for a much more refined analysis of multiple, interacting variables specific to a particular farm. For example, precision farmers connect computers and global positioning devices to their combines when harvesting a crop to obtain a precise map of variations in yield, almost to the square meter. They may obtain infrared maps of their farm from satellites or aircraft. They use these data when planting and maintaining their crops. For example, the equipment used to plant, fertilize, and water the crops—again, equipped with computers and global positioning devices—permits farmers to vary regimens precisely to the specific conditions of each unique area of their farms. By systematically noting the interactions among a wide range of variables, precision farmers share with one another the effects of diverse and complexly interacting variables that not only help them increase their yields but also deepen theoretical understandings about crop science that might be applied across diverse farms. Precision farming also depends on collaboration across various disciplines, categories of expertise, and technologies including soil and crop sciences, computer technology, meteorology, genetics, chemistry, and satellite and infrared technologies to allow farmers to bring all of these diverse resources together in a manageable way.

We hope the analogy to education and literacy research and to the potential role of formative and design experiments is obvious. Successful farming entails contending with an incredibly complex array of interacting variables that are often unique to an individual farm. Successful teaching is more complex and perhaps more localized. Conventional experimental methodologies in education and literacy research may produce broad generalizations that, although useful in a general sense, do not permit the fine-grained information most helpful to an individual teacher working in a particular classroom. Neither do conventional experimental methodologies provide much power or depth in teasing out complexly interacting variables that may have substantive and sometimes unpredictable effects on how an instructional intervention does or doesn't work—or what to do when it isn't working. Conventional naturalistic methodologies drawing on qualitative data may provide richer descriptive data, but those data are rarely aimed specifically at identifying which factors enhance or inhibit the utility of a specific intervention.

The precision farming analogy also highlights the utility of interdisciplinary collaborations and multiple methodological and theoretical perspectives in understanding and transforming practice. Nonetheless, it also reveals some of the limitations of and unanswered questions about formative and design experiments. For example, how does this approach deal with making the data and findings from intense involvement in one or a few carefully selected environments useful to a broad range of practitioners?

Taken together, these examples highlight some key themes that are closely associated with a rationale for including formative and design experiments as a domain of research within the education and literacy research literature:

- Formative and design experiments are grounded in developing understanding by seeking to accomplish practical and useful educational goals.
- They are focused on less controlled, authentic environments instead of tightly controlled laboratory-like settings.

- They use and develop theory in the context of trying to engineer successful instructional interventions. Thus, they dwell in the realm of engineering science rather than social science.
- They entail innovative and speculative experimentation.
- They are interdisciplinary, employing multiple theoretical and methodological perspectives and orientations.
- They seek understandings that accommodate many complex, interacting variables in diverse contexts.
- They seek generalizations from multiple examples rather than from random samples and controlled experimentation.

In subsequent sections of this chapter, we delve more specifically into the rationale for and the origins of formative and design experiments and how literacy researchers might conceptualize them. Each section introduces a question about formative and design experiments. We imagined these questions to be among those a doctoral student who wished to conduct a formative or design experiment for a dissertation study might be asked by committee members unfamiliar with formative or design experiments. That organizational frame seemed appropriate to us, because we see current doctoral students as central to the audience for this series of books on methodologies for literacy research.

In fact, to reinforce the points made thus far, and as a transition to a more specific discussion, we imagined several doctoral students who are each interested in studying some aspect of reading comprehension instruction. We imagined them all being asked how they selected a question and methodology for their dissertation. The first two students respond that they selected a research question consistent with a methodological stance dictated by their worldviews. One student, who is oriented toward pinning down reality in a concrete world of numerical measures and who sees a researcher's role as a dispassionate collector of data, decides to conduct a scientific experiment comparing two approaches to teaching comprehension strategies with a control group that will receive no strategy instruction. That student will use carefully selected quantitative measures of comprehension and statistical analyses. The second student, who sees a researcher's role as an ideologically positioned interpreter of an essentially social world, will conduct a qualitative study of the extent to which comprehension instruction is influenced by the administrative and professional climate of the school. We believe that these two students are representative of the most common stances of literacy researchers today in selecting a methodology. That is, loyalty to, preference for, or at least past experience with a methodology dictates the questions and issues they pursue, the theoretical frameworks they employ, and so forth. In other words, methodology is the starting point for their research agendas and questions.

A third student does not start with a preferred research methodology but instead heeds the advice of a trusted mentor who cautioned: "If all you have is a hammer, everything looks like a nail." That is, as Howe (1988) stated, "why should paradigms [i.e., worldviews] determine the kind of work one may do with inquiry any more than the amount of illumination should determine where one may conduct a search" (p. 13). In that view, the nature of a research question and the search for all available avenues to answering it should be the starting point for selecting a methodological approach. For example, this student may want to address not only which approach to comprehension is more effective but also which is more appealing to administrators, teachers, and students—and why. Given that question, the student might consider collecting survey data, qualitative data in the form of interviews, quantitative analyses including correlations between comprehension achievement scores and survey results, and so forth. This student is perhaps representative of a growing interest in mixed methods among education researchers (e.g., Chatterji, 2004).

A fourth student's starting point is more in the spirit of Pasteur, Edison, the Wright brothers, and modern test pilots. That is, the starting point for this student's dissertation study is a desire to see how a promising classroom intervention grounded in theory can be successfully implemented in the real world of practice. Or the student may want to create a viable theory-driven intervention for achieving a valued pedagogical goal. For example, this student might be interested in determining if and how the positive effects of an approach to comprehension instruction tested under carefully controlled conditions could be replicated when all the naturally occurring variations in classrooms are allowed to operate freely. Or the student may wish to test an innovative intervention aimed at achieving a critical or problematic goal of comprehension instruction, such as promoting critical reading. The questions guiding the research include: (1) Do the theoretical underpinnings of the intervention stand up to actual classroom practice? (2) What factors enhance or inhibit the intervention's effectiveness and how might the intervention be modified accordingly (thus the terms *formative* and *design*)? (3) Does implementing the intervention reveal the need to modify existing theory or to create new theory? (4) What unexpected collateral effects might the intervention precipitate?

Formative and design experiments are an approach to research that accommodates this more engineering stance toward education research, and thus they promote attention to a different category of questions that bring research and practice closely together. This approach to research tests theory and the results from more controlled studies in the crucible of classroom practice. In the remainder of this chapter we position this emerging approach to research more explicitly within the methodological landscape of education research, and we answer some key foundational questions about its conceptualization and use.

1.1. How Do Formative and Design Experiments Fit into the Methodological Landscape and Where Did They Come From?

In this section we trace the roots of formative and design experiments and how the underlying rationale and perspectives of this approach to research relate to conventional, mainstream research methods. We show that this approach to research is still emerging, but that its origins and use included highly regarded literacy researchers. First, we discuss key terms associated with this approach and how its diverse terminology reflects an evolution of understandings and interpretations among researchers from different fields and disciplines in education.

1.1.1. What terms have been used to describe this approach to research?

It was not easy to settle on the terminology to use in this book. The approach to research that we have termed *formative and design experiments* has been referred to using a variety of other terms, including *formative research* (Reigeluth & Frick, 1999), *design studies, teaching experiments* (Kelley & Lesh, 2000), *development research* (van den Akker, 1999), *design-based research* (Design-Based Research Collective, 2003), and *lesson studies* (Lewis, Perry, & Murata, 2006). A recent book containing the work of a group of international scholars interested in this approach (van den Akker et al., 2006) uses the term *design research* in its title, although some of its contributors use other terminology. These and other like-minded researchers have also promoted the legitimacy of this new approach to research as the basis for a new field referred to as *learning sciences.* It remains to be seen whether a single term for this relatively new approach to research will dominate and whether well-specified frameworks, methods, and standards of rigor will solidify, or whether perhaps several models for conducting research in this new vein will exist around a common core of principles, much like conventional quantitative and qualitative methodologies for research include a variety of methodological and analytical approaches that are all considered legitimate.

This diversity of terms and the lack of clear consensus about terminology reflect several important points about this approach to research. First, it is indicative of its roots among researchers in diverse disciplines and methodological backgrounds. Second, it reflects the relative methodological infancy of this approach and an as yet incomplete methodological evolution. Third, because different terms have emerged from different sources, it reflects the conceptual appeal of this approach to researchers from diverse backgrounds and disciplines in education who are nonetheless united in their search for research methods better suited to positively transforming instruction and to more directly informing practice. Fourth, it reflects the methodological flexibility and the diversity of frameworks that have been characteristic of its use.

Despite the diversity of terminology, we decided to use the collective term *formative and design experiments* for several reasons. First, we think the use of that term pays homage to the seminal articulation of this new approach by Ann Brown (1992), Allan Collins (1992), and Dennis Newman (1990; see also Jacob, 1992). These researchers described their work as either design experiments or formative experiments. The terms *formative* and *design* also reflect two fundamental aspects of this approach to research: (1) the work of a researcher using this approach is fundamentally to design an instructional intervention that works to achieve a valued pedagogical goal in an authentic classroom environment. (2) Doing so implies modifying the intervention formatively in response to data suggesting factors that enhance or inhibit the intervention's effectiveness, efficiency, and appeal.

We also believe that linking the individual terms *formative experiment* and *design experiment* reflects the subtle, but important, differences in emphases among researchers who prefer one or the other term, even if these terms have essentially the same conceptual roots. In our view, researchers who gravitate toward the term *design experiment* tend to see their work more directly as an extension of conventional laboratory work grounded in quantitative methods. They are also more interested in creating a *design science* that claims legitimacy by using conventional views of causation and generalization. For example, some researchers see design experiments as essentially a precursor to more conventional randomized trials using quantitative methods (e.g, Gersten, 2005; McCandliss, Kalchman, & Bryant, 2003). Those who gravitate toward the use of the term *formative experiment*, on the other hand, tend to be guided by a more local, less formalized workability grounded in a more pragmatic and qualitative stance. They see their work as legitimate and useful independent of any contribution it may make to conventional methodologies and as geared more toward informing practitioners than to creating a design science. They are less concerned about establishing specific causal relations, and they view generalization more broadly than simply extrapolating findings from a sample to a population.

To our knowledge, Newman (1992) is the only writer who tried to make a clear distinction between the two terms:

> Our formative experiments . . . differ from the design experiments proposed by Collins [1992] in this volume. Our work has been less systematic than will be necessary for establishing a design science, and the observations are done by the same group of people responsible for development. In other respects the point of view is very similar, e.g., the focus on the whole environment as the unit of analysis. Our observations thus provide hypotheses that a design science can pursue. (p. 64)

The term *design experiment* clearly has been the preferred term among most education researchers. However, it is interesting to note that literacy researchers have more often used the term *formative experiment*, which also explains why we include it in our terminology. Nonetheless, there are exceptions to these broad characterizations and much common ground between those who use the term *formative experiment* and those who use *design experiment*. Thus, we believe it is reasonable to consider these terms to be more or less equivalent in this book and at least representative of an approach to research that has been conducted using a variety of related terms.

Contrary to recent trends in terminology, we have also retained the term *experiment*, although that term entails some potential misunderstandings. For example, it may lead some to consider this approach to be a form of the experimental method, which it is decidedly not. That may explain why some researchers have dropped the term *experiment* when describing this approach. However, we believe that using the term *experiment* emphasizes that a central activity of this approach is akin to developing an experimental aircraft that is systematically tested and modified accordingly. A more practical, and less noble, reason is that we believe the term *experiment* has a positive connotation among those in governmental agencies who privilege a conventional scientific paradigm in making funding decisions but who see design *experiments* as a type of pilot study or crude precursor to conducting more rigorous and more highly valued randomized field trials (often referred to as the *gold standard* of education research). On the other hand, we hope that this book will contribute to dispelling that misconception.

There are other issues of terminology that are beyond the scope of this book. For example, is it more appropriate to refer to formative and design experiments as an *approach* to research, as a research *method* or set of methods, or as a research *methodology*. (See Kelly, 2004, for a discussion of this issue in regard to design experiments and Kamberelis & Dimitriadis, 2004, an earlier book in this series, in regard to literacy research). To sidestep some of those complicated, though important, issues in this book, we refer to formative and design experiments as an approach to research, although we believe it might also qualify as a methodology.

1.1.2. What are the defining characteristics of formative and design experiments?

Despite the differing terminology noted in the previous section, there is considerable agreement about the defining characteristics of formative and design experiments. However, any specification of this approach's defining characteristics reflects more of a general perspective or orientation than a set list of criteria to be applied prescriptively to every investigation or to be used in determining precisely whether a study is a legitimate example. The following are some relevant quotes that set the stage for a listing of defining characteristics (all emphases are in the originals):

> Design based research is, by necessity a manifold enterprise with regard to research focus, practice, and underlying epistemology . . . [it is a] high-level methodological orientation. (Bell, 2004, p. 245)

> Design-based research is not so much *an* approach as it is a series of approaches, with the intent of producing new theories, artifacts, and practices that account for and potentially impact learning and teaching in naturalistic settings. (Barab & Squire, 2004, p. 2)

> I do not think it is . . . productive to spend much time trying to come up with a simple account that ends all controversy about *what design experiments really are*—there is no right answer. For there *is no one thing that they are like.* (Phillips, 2006, p. 94)

Despite this lack of specificity among researchers interested in this approach, there is some convergence about its defining characteristics. And the fewer of these characteristics that are evident, the less likely it is that a researcher is operating within the general parameters of this approach. We offer the following list of defining characteristics, drawing on published work by Cobb and colleagues (2003a, who refer to "crosscutting features of design experiments," p. 9); Collins (1999); Jacob (1992); and on our own work (Baumann, Dillen, Schockley, Alverman, & Reinking, 1996; Reinking & Bradley, 2004; Reinking & Pickle, 1993; and Reinking & Watkins, 1998).

1. Intervention-centered in authentic instructional contexts. The central object of study in a formative or design experiment is always an instructional intervention, broadly defined. Thus, formative and design experiments are fundamentally intervention research. According to Sandoval (2004), an intervention is an "embodied conjecture . . . about how theoretical propositions might be reified within designed environments to support learning" (p. 215). The intervention is often innovative and often aims to address a problematic area of instruction or to positively transform instruction. On the other hand, the intervention may be one that is well known and that has been investigated extensively using other methodologies. It might be a single well-defined instructional activity or a coherent set of activities aimed at accomplishing well-defined goals. In any event, to be a formative or design experiment, the intervention must be studied in an authentic instructional environment where all naturally occurring variation is allowed to operate and where instructional responses to that variation are not unnaturally constrained by the researcher. In Chapter 3 we give some examples from literacy research.

2. Theoretical. Formative and design experiments are guided by theory, but theory plays a different role than in other approaches to research. The examples of Pasteur, Edison, and the Wright brothers offered in the introduction to this chapter illustrate to some extent the role of theory in formative and design experiments. For example, the Wright brothers used long-standing theories to achieve lift, but they developed new theories about how to control flight, which was the ultimate goal of their project. Similarly, as Cobb and colleagues (2003a) stated, the purpose of design experiments is "to develop a class of theories about both the *process* of learning and the *means* that are designed to support learning" (p. 9, emphasis in the original). Further, they state that in developing theories "design experiments create conditions . . . [that] place these theories in harm's way" and that theory "must do real work" by being *"accountable to the activity of design"* (p. 10, emphasis added; see also Bell, 2004). Further, they describe the theories that emerge from design experiments as humble and local in contrast to more grandiose, overarching explanatory theories, although the latter may be used to guide the implementation of an intervention. For example, theories of motivation about reading may be used to create, implement, and refine an intervention aimed at increasing independent reading, and a formative experiment may provide data documenting the utility or limitations of motivation theory in practice. However, a researcher using this approach is often more focused on discovering pedagogical theories that capture categories of factors that enhance or inhibit the effectiveness of the instructional intervention in achieving its goal. For example, in our own work (Reinking & Watkins, 2000) with students creating computer-based, multimedia book reviews, we found that students incidentally shared much information about the books they were reading in the context of helping each other learn the technological techniques for designing the multimedia reviews.

In their extensive discussion of the role of theory in design experiments, diSessa and Cobb (2004) suggested that such findings are the grist for what they call "ontological innovation," where pedagogical findings in the context of a design experiment "validate a new category of existence" (p. 84). For example, in their work, they introduced the term *meta-representational competence* to capture a set of factors that were critical in introducing physics concepts to elementary school students. Importantly, this attention to theory is a defining characteristic that separates formative and design experiments from related research activities such as formative evaluation, which is more aimed at workability alone. That is, formative and design experiments are not aimed only at creating conditions that allow an intervention to accomplish a pedagogical goal. Instead, they are also aimed at theoretically understanding the conditions that enhance or inhibit an intervention's effectiveness and at generating pedagogical understandings that generalize beyond specific instances (see Tabak, 2004) and specifically that can inform practitioners.

3. Goal oriented. Formative and design experiments investigate explicitly and directly how to improve education and learning in authentic educational settings. Thus, defining what improvement is sought and why it is necessary may be central to conceptualizing, conducting, and reporting formative and design experiments, as we noted in our previous example of an imaginary doctoral student's decision to conduct a formative or design experiment as a dissertation study. A researcher using this approach to research will, more often than other researchers, explicitly articulate a goal of the intervention and why it is important. Further, that explicit goal becomes a day-to-day reference point for collecting and analyzing data, for making modifications to the intervention (see the subsequent characteristic), and at the end of the investigation for determining the extent to which progress has been made. Because formative and design experiments are aimed at improving practice, the rationale for a goal's importance is inherent to establishing the rationale for an investigation. The goal may be important because it addresses an intractable instructional problem, a gap in the curriculum, a neglected area of instruction, and so forth. An example of a goal that fits these categories among literacy educators would be improving students' ability to read critically (see Purcell-Gates, 2006). Justifying the goal's importance may also imply an explicit statement of values. Why exactly is critical reading important? Is developing it more important than other literacy goals. Other approaches to research do not address such value-laden issues directly, because instruction goals in other methodologies and approaches are often assumed or are subordinate to testing a theory or looking through a particular theoretical or ideological lens.

4. Adaptive and iterative. Researchers who use conventional experiments to study the effectiveness of interventions in classrooms must contend with the issue of fidelity. That is, to strengthen the internal validity of their findings, they must ensure that the intervention of interest is carried out according to precise specifications within each lesson, classroom, and school in the experiment. Typically, that is not easy to do, and it is contrary to the natural inclinations of educators who understand that it is often necessary to adapt instruction to particular circumstances. Further, if the findings for the intervention are statistically favorable, a researcher can only claim that that the intervention is effective in general when enacted precisely as implemented in the experiment. This need for fidelity contributes to the gap between research findings and the demands of authentic practice, because findings say little about what circumstances enhance or inhibit the intervention's workability and effectiveness.

Fidelity is the antithesis of formative and design experiments. A researcher using this approach begins with the assumption that the intervention that is implemented at the beginning of an investigation may be substantially different by the end of the investigation, because the main goal of the research is to adapt the intervention to make it work better in response to the inherent variability within classrooms. That is, data are collected to determine what is and is not working and why, and then the intervention is adapted accordingly. This process is typically iterative either in microcycles within a classroom or in macrocycles across classrooms and studies (see Gravemeijer & Cobb, 2006). The intervention is like a prototype that is continuously tested and tweaked to improve its performance, much like an experimental aircraft or like Edison experimenting with different materials to use as the filament in a lightbulb. For example, a literacy researcher may find that struggling readers respond differently to an intervention because it draws other students' attention to their difficulties, leading to a reframing of how the intervention is presented and carried out. This adaptive and iterative approach is what good teachers do, but rarely do teachers have the opportunity or resources to gather systematic, rigorous data in service of the deep insights that process might produce.

5. Transformative. As noted in item 1, an intervention that is the object of a formative or design experiment is often one that has the potential to positively transform the environment for teaching and learning. Interventions most worthy of study are those that address pedagogical goals that are valued and worthy of study, perhaps because they extend teaching and learning in important directions, fill a gap in the curriculum, respond to difficult instructional problems, and so forth. Further, formative and design experiments are often guided by the realization that the intervention and its implementation within a particular context may produce important unintended consequences, many of which may contribute to theory building and to ideas for further research. For example, a literacy researcher might expect an intervention to change the way teachers conceptualizes literacy instruction, what they emphasize, the way they structure their lessons, or the physical layout of their classrooms. Or a researcher might expect students to shift their orientations to textual information in other content areas. At the same time, a researcher is sensitive to what positive or negative unanticipated effects the intervention may produce.

6. Methodologically inclusive and flexible. Unlike other dominant research methodologies in education research, conceptualizing and conducting formative and design experiments are not driven mainly by a particular method of collecting and analyzing data (Bell, 2004). Any approach to data collection and analysis may be appropriate to formative and design experiments if a researcher can justify how it furthers understanding about the effects of the intervention and how it might be implemented more effectively, or how it might help refine theory. Likewise, approaches to data collection and analysis may be adapted in response to developments during an investigation. For example, a literacy researcher may collect baseline quantitative data on reading achievement or motivation to read by using standardized or experimenter-developed instruments and make statistical comparisons before and after the intervention is implemented. However, because the intent of formative and design experiments is to understand contextual factors that influence the effectiveness of an intervention, this approach must entail collecting and analyzing qualitative data. Qualitative data are needed because this approach to research falls clearly into what Salomon (1991) has called systemic rather than analytic research. Thus, formative and design experiments are clearly compatible with mixed methods and the attendant concerns, advantages, and standards of rigor associated with that research methodology (see Chatterji, 2004; Johnson & Onwuegbuzie, 2004; Tashakkori & Teddlie, 1998).

7. *Pragmatic.* Stanovich (2000) argued that scientists and teachers are similarly pragmatic in seeking knowledge that works without engaging in deeper philosophical musings about what entails truth. Formative and design experiments represent an approach particularly consistent with that view. Researchers who gravitate toward this approach focus on creating conditions that allow promising interventions to work, and they seek theory that can be directly useful to practitioners. They are not interested in debating philosophical question about ultimate meanings. They focus on what Messick (1992) called consequential validity, where results have demonstrable value in improving instruction. That view is consistent with the philosophy of pragmatism. In subsequent sections, particularly Section 1.3, we will discuss how pragmatism is a philosophy that can justify formative and design experiments and how literacy researchers have been encouraged to embrace this view in their work (Dillon, O'Brien, & Heilman, 2000).

1.1.3. How do formative and design experiments compare to other approaches to investigating interventions in classrooms?

The most common methodologies for investigating instruction in classrooms have been among the various approaches within the broad categories of scientific experimentation or naturalistic inquiry. Formative and design experiments do not fit neatly into either category. So how are they different from these more conventional methodologies and approaches? A succinct response is represented in Figure 1.2. Interestingly, after developing that figure, we discovered a similar figure that Harste (1993) developed many years ago and published in his commentary on the limitations of meta-analysis in literacy research and the risks of overselling experimental research in the formulation of educational policy. In that article he pointed out that he was trained as an experimental researcher but that he came to reject that approach in favor of a view that went beyond experimental and naturalistic inquiry and that conceptualized research as a "formalized version of the learning process" (p. 357). He termed this view of research "collaborative." For comparison, we present his original figure here as Figure 1.3.

Formative and design experiments do share common ground with other approaches to research. However, this common ground can lead to some confusion about the essential elements of formative and design experiments and how they are different from other, more familiar methodologies and approaches. For example, when we describe our own studies as *formative experiments,* many of our colleagues ask if our work is akin to *formative evaluation.* The answer is "yes and no." Like the formative evaluation often exercised in the development of an instructional product, formative and design experiments focus on workability and fine-tuning a beta version in light of systematic data collection. However, unlike formative evaluation, they are more grounded in theory and theory development as well as the desire to understand why an intervention does or doesn't work. As the Design-Based Research Collective (2003) stated,

> Design-based research goes beyond merely designing and testing particular interventions. Interventions embody specific theoretical claims about teaching and learning, and reflect a commitment to understanding the relationships among theory, designed artifacts, and practice. (p. 6)

Similarly, Cobb and colleagues (2003a; see also Shavelson, Phillips, Towne, & Feur, 2003) explained that in design experiments

> "What works" is underpinned by a concern for "how, when, and why" it works, and by a detailed specification of what exactly, "it" is. This intimate relationship between the development and theory and the improvement of instructional design for bringing about new forms of learning is a hallmark of the design experiment methodology. (p. 13)

Figure 1.2. A comparison of formative and design experiments to conventional methodologies

	Methodology/Approach		
	Experimental	Naturalistic	Formative/Design
Contextual variation	Controlled, or viewed as nuisance and neutralized by randomization	Studied, analyzed	Studied, analyzed, accommodated
Dominant metaphor(s)	Laboratory	Lens, rhizome, jazz	Ecology, engineering
Guiding question	What is best most of the time?	What is?	What could be?
Stance toward intervention	Comparison (x vs. y)	Sociocultural and ideologically positioned practice	Selection (x or y) and modification ($x^1 \rightarrow x^2 \rightarrow x^3 \rightarrow x^4 \rightarrow$etc.)
Operative goal	Establish causal relations	Generate thick descriptions	Put theory to work
Utility	Broad generalizations across contexts, top-down policy making	Nuanced understanding, raised consciousness, ideological confirmation, social action	Context-specific recommendations; identifies factors and mechanisms enabling effective practice
Philosophy/stance (epistemology)	Positivism, postpositivism, scientific realism	Constructivism	Pragmatism
Theoretical imperative	General laws and reductionist models	Deep sociocultural understandings	Workability
Methodological imperative	Internal validity (fidelity)	Interpretative trustworthiness	Ecological validity
Participants	Pawns	Agents	Partners
Prototypical researcher	Chess-playing statistician	Butterfly-chasing ethnographer	Deal-making, mixed methodologist
Starting point for research	Theory-driven question or hypothesis rooted in a quest for attainable truth	Theory-driven question rooted in sociocultural awareness	Pedagogical goal connecting theory and practice rooted in values
Relations and contributions to practice	Broad generalizations	Deep reflections	Specific suggestions

Figure 1.3. Changing views of research

Research Perspectives	Experimental	Naturalistic	Collaborative
Focus	Comprehension	Interpretation	Learning
Vehicle	Prediction	Description	Collaboration
Intent	Add credence	Uncover theories of meaning	Interrogating assumptions and beliefs
Researcher's stance	*I* prioritized	*I–you* visible	*We* vulnerable
Stance on knowledge	Fixed	Contextual	Relational
Procedure	Test hypotheses	Multiple perspectives	Tensions and anomalies
Methodological stance	Innocent	Relative	Democratic
Path to understanding	Simplicity	Complexity	Reflexivity
Role of research relative to schooling in our society	Cultural literacy	Cultural diversity	Morality
How significance is determined	Individual	Cooperative	Collaborative
Results	Better or cleaner arguments	More complex explanations	Learning and new invitations to inquiry
Presentational form	Report	Story	Invitation
Product	Study	Thick description	Journey

Source: Harste, 1993.

Unlike formative evaluation, formative and design experiments are also more attuned to the role of the social context in determining what factors enhance or inhibit an intervention's effectiveness, and the intervention is viewed as a socially constructed object (see Bannan-Ritland, 2003). In formative experiments, as Jacob (1992) stated,

> Researchers [modify] the materials or the *social organization* to bring about the desired goal. The approaches [use] traditional ethnographic methods, such as participant observations and videotaping,

to identify problems, to propose possible solutions, and to document before, during, and after change. (p. 322, emphasis added)

Likewise, in regard to theory development, formative and design experiments go beyond evaluation studies, although we wish to note that it is not clear what evaluation studies actually are or the extent to which they must have a theoretical base to be rigorously conducted (see Reinking & Alvermann, 2005). Again, quoting the Design-Based Research Collective (2003):

> Evaluators often conceptualize context as a set of factors that are independent of the intervention itself but that may influence its effects . . . unlike evaluation research, design-based research views a successful innovation as a joint product of the designed intervention and the context. . . . Models, rather than particular artifacts or programs, are the goal. . . . The value of attending to context is not simply that it produces a better understanding of an intervention, but also that it can lead to improved theoretical accounts of teaching and learning. In this sense design-based research differs from evaluation research in the ways context and intervention are problematized. (p. 7)

Formative and design experiments are also similar to but different from *action research* or *teacher research* (Reason & Bradbury, 2001). Both approaches put complex variability in everyday instructional contexts at the center of conducting research. Both may address valued instructional goals as a starting point for research projects, and both have a pragmatic orientation to research, including pragmatism's focus on democratic values (see Section 1.3). Nonetheless, there are important differences. Action research has a more explicit ideological emphasis focused on issues of power, and research is viewed as a means of emancipating participants from limitations imposed by race, class, gender, ability, and age (Arhar, Holly, & Kasten, 2001). Professional maturation, development, and empowerment are also central to action research. Formative and design experiments often lead to similar enhancements, but they do so more incidentally. Likewise, teachers assume the role of researcher in action research (see Tafel & Fischer, 2001), but their involvement in formative or design experiments is more typically as a valued informant, although they may choose to become part of the research team (see Section 2.5).

Theory development in action research is secondary at best. For example, Reason and Bradbury (2001) stated,

> The primary purpose of action research is not to produce academic theories based on action; nor is it to produce theories about action; nor is it to produce theoretical or empirical knowledge that can be applied to action; it is to liberate the human body, mind and spirit in the search for a better, freer world. (p. 2)

Formative and design experiments also share common ground with *activity theory,* which is more a theoretical viewpoint than an approach to research. Activity theory, which has been employed by literacy researchers (e.g., Beach, 2000), originated in studies investigating the workplace (see Engeström, Miettinen, & Punamäki, 1998). This theory suggests that change in work environments can only be brought about through acknowledging and understanding the relation among the sociohistorical context, the objects and tools that are integral to the work environment, and the social interactions that mediate their use. Nonetheless, activity theory is more focused on what is, rather than what could be.

These approaches, when taken together with formative and design experiments, reveal a long-standing conceptual and methodological dissatisfaction with narrow interpretations and applications of scientific experimentation or naturalistic inquiry in education research in general and literacy research in particular. Such narrow perspectives centered in methodological purity and a preoccupation with abstract, general theories do not fit well with the complexity of teaching and learning in classrooms, and the frequent debates about them have distracted the field from focusing on research that more directly informs practice (Dillon et al., 2000). Harste's (1993) views, captured in Figure 1.3, expressed that dissatisfaction and distraction, foreshadowing the dominant themes underlying formative and design experiments and the need to find approaches to research that better serve the needs of the field. In the next section, we present an overview of how the origins of formative and design experiments reflect education researchers', particularly prominent literacy researchers', search for more authentic and meaningful approaches to research.

1.1.4. What is the origin of formative and design experiments?

We have compared answering this question to finding the source of a river formed by the convergence of many streams (Reinking & Bradley, 2004). The earliest manifestations of the perspectives, orientations, and research methods associated with formative and design experiments can be traced to researchers from diverse traditions and interests.

The earliest ideas and perspectives leading to formative and design experiments appeared in the 1980s, although these perspectives and ideas did not coalesce into a definite approach to research until the early 1990s. Jacob (1992) attributes the term and this new design to neo-Vygotskian scholars' dissatisfaction with the lack of ecological validity in conventional experiments and with descriptive studies that "can tell us about the current forms and content of schooling and larger societal influences on schooling, [but that] tell us little about what *could* be" (pp. 320–321, emphasis in original). She goes on to suggest that formative experiments arose in part from the work of cognitive psychologists, guided by a Vygotskian perspective, investigating how cognitive tasks could be influenced by the context in which the task took place, citing particularly the work of Newman, Griffin, and Cole (1989). Denis Newman's (1990) report of a study aimed at using computer-based activities to transform the teaching and learning of science concepts was arguably the first study to be designed specifically as a formative experiment and was one of the first to outline the parameters of formative experiments as an approach to research.

The early work of Luis Moll and his colleagues in the 1980s (Diaz, Moll, & Mehan, 1986; Moll & Diaz, 1987) also had elements suggestive of formative and design experiments, although they did not use that terminology. Moll, a researcher interested in problematic aspects of literacy development among Spanish-speaking students in bilingual programs, used ethnographic methods and case studies to define relevant dimensions of instruction and then modify the instructional environment in order to ameliorate problems. The title of Moll and Diaz's 1987 article reporting these results highlighted a central theme of formative and design experiments: "Change as the Goal of Educational Research."

It is not clear exactly how the term *design experiment* arose in relation to *formative experiment,* but its origins can be traced to

publications by Ann Brown (1992), Alan Collins (1992), and Denis Newman (1992). Brown's 1992 article seems to be the first use
and explication of the term in a peer-reviewed outlet, and it is
often cited as the seminal source for this approach to research.
However, in that article she credits Collins with the term by citing
his then in-press chapter (Collins, 1992). Collins, in a later publication (1999), cites both his early-published chapter and Brown's
article in reference to the origin of design experiments and its
methodological roots. Newman's (1992) chapter on formative experiments acknowledges Collins's (1992) chapter in the same edited book, and he addresses both the similarities and differences
between formative and design experiments. Clearly, the work of
these three scholars was instrumental, if not foundational, in formulating and promoting design experiments.

Brown's adoption of this approach to research in her work
is particularly important in tracing the origins of formative and
design experiments for another reason. She was a highly regarded experimental educational psychologist well established in the
mainstream of education research. It is also noteworthy in the
context of this book that her work was highly regarded and influential among literacy researchers, given her focus on the metacognitive aspects of reading comprehension and her exploration
of the implications of her laboratory research for mainstream
reading instruction in classrooms. In that regard, she is a prime
example in the best tradition of educational psychologists who,
especially during the 1980s, became interested not only in testing
theory in highly controlled laboratory settings but also in translating theory and laboratory research into specific activities for
instructional practice.

It is historically interesting to note that formative and design
experiments have been an avenue for many researchers trained
in conventional experimental methods to embrace qualitative
methods in their work. For example, Brown (1992) describes how
she progressed from her roots as a classical learning theorist to
designing experiments in classroom settings. Though trained to
study subjects in strictly controlled laboratory settings, she and
other researchers began to acknowledge "the fact that real-life
learning inevitably takes place in a social context" (p. 144). Further, as there was a shift in the importance of the contexts in which
learning occurred, there was also a shift in what was to be learned

and how it would be assessed. Consequently, there developed a need to consider new and more complex methodologies.

Brown also strongly advocated the use of video in determining the contextual factors that influence efforts to implement instructional interventions in classrooms. This case of a prolific and insightful researcher seeing the limitations of conventional experimental methods reflects a path to awareness that other researchers have followed independently, including the first author of this book.

Brown (1992) was also instructive and enlightening in introducing some of the foundational themes and issues associated with design and formative experiments. These themes and issues include (1) an acknowledgment of the need for methods that allow for studying the morass of variations that occur in classrooms; (2) the need for interdisciplinary perspectives and collaboration among researchers, teachers, and students to create learning communities; (3) the complementarity of laboratory and design experiments, particularly in relation to generating and building theory; (4) the need to determine what factors contribute to enabling "an effective intervention to migrate from our experimental classroom to average classrooms operated by average students and teachers" (p. 143); (5) the blurring of basic and applied research; and (6) the need for data collection and analysis that can inform practice. She also employed a metaphor likely to appeal to those with a scientific bent:

> My agenda is more like that of a designer or engineer. I need to unconfound variables, not only for theoretical clarity, but also so that necessary and sufficient aspects of the intervention can be disseminated. The question becomes, what are the absolutely essential features that must be in place to cause change under conditions that one can reasonably hope to exist in normal school settings. (p. 173)

Designing Classroom Research: Themes, Issues, and Struggles (Eisenkart & Borko, 1993) reflected the methodological zeitgeist in educational research during the early 1990s, which created fertile ground for the emergence of formative and design experiments. The authors, an anthropologist of education and an educational psychologist, did not refer directly to formative and design experiments, but they did promote many of the fundamental themes underlying that approach and made a strong argument for methodological flexibility and innovation in classroom research. For example, they argued that "educational research is evolving; its designs and procedures are not cast in stone. Conscientious researchers are continually trying out new methods . . . to make their work stronger, more compelling, and more useful" (p. 11). In fact, we believe that the theoretical, methodological, and practical issues and perspectives that Eisenhart and Borko presented and the methodological frameworks and standards of rigor they offered come close to being a manual for designing and conducting classroom research in general and formative and design experiments in particular. For example, they argue for the following:

1. Classroom researchers should try to design research studies that accommodate the complexity and distinctiveness of classroom life.
2. Comprehensiveness can be enhanced through efforts at interdisciplinary collaboration.
3. Research comprehensiveness, as well as the value of research for practice, can be enhanced through efforts to engage teachers and researchers in more complementary research roles.
4. Classroom research should be conceived in the spirit of ongoing deliberation, negotiation, and decision making by all interested parties.
5. Classroom research should be conducted in accord with some agreed-upon standards of validity.
6. Classroom researchers should intend specifically to design their research so its results can be used to address important issues of educational practice.
7. Classroom researchers and teachers should make long-term commitments to the study and improvement of classroom practices. (pp. 131–134)

Electronic Quills: A Situated Evaluation of Using Computers for Classroom Writing (Bruce & Rubin, 1993), published in the same year, also drew conclusions and offered perspectives consistent with the rationale for formative and design experiments. The authors, both prominent literary researchers, reported their extensive classroom efforts across several years to develop and implement QUILL, a computer program designed to engage students in more authentic purposes for reading and writing. Stimulated in part by their growing realization that teachers were not implementing computer-based intervention in ways consistent with the intent of the program, they adopted a different methodological stance toward their research. They called that stance *situated evaluation*, which entailed many of the features associated today with formative and design experiments. In their view, situated evaluation was an alternative to formative and summative evaluations, because the latter approaches placed an innovative instructional intervention at the center of an investigation and treated the instructional environment as an idealized environment and a passive system. Instead, situated evaluation focused more on the situational context, and attempts to implement the intervention are viewed as a process of integration with potentially unexpected outcomes. Another distinguishing feature of situated evaluation is that the focus is on why an intervention does or does not produce desired results, not simply how the innovation can be modified to work better. In situated evaluation, the researcher's role is also separate from the developer's role. As they stated,

> The developers may intend that the innovation modify the social system so that certain desirable characteristics are achieved. They see the innovation set in an idealized context and used in an idealized way. Their vision of the changed social system is thus an *idealization*. What happens in practice is that the social system may or may not change at all, and if it does change, it may not do so in accord with the developers' goals. . . . The distinction between the ideal and the real is a process, the *realization process*. (p. 198, emphasis in original)

The diversity of these sources, often arising independently among researchers from different methodological traditions and with diverse research interests, illustrates how researchers committed to understanding and to transforming teaching and learning in real classrooms have found conventional research methodologies inadequate and how they have searched for alternatives. It also illustrates that these urges have been particularly strong among literacy researchers. Formative and design experiments (or what has been termed *design research*, as explained in Section 1.1.1) represent the most coherent manifestation of an approach to research that addresses these urges. In the following section we discuss in more detail a rationale for why formative and design experiments are needed and how this approach meets the needs of the field.

1.2. WHY ARE FORMATIVE AND
DESIGN EXPERIMENTS NEEDED AND USEFUL?

This is an important and reasonable question that we believe should be answered explicitly for any approach to education and literacy research. The need for and usefulness of more conventional methodologies, particularly in relation to their advantages and limitations in improving educational practice, are rarely made explicit. If those who embrace other research methodologies and approaches responded directly to this question, it would, we believe, reveal limitations that make the need for formative and design experiments more obvious.

However, researchers using more conventional methodologies are not likely to question the need for or usefulness of their preferred methodology. As we noted in the introduction to this chapter, some researchers' transcendent worldviews are compatible only with a single methodology (e.g., Guba & Lincoln, 1994; Stanovich, 2000). They are unlikely to see the limitations of their preferred methodology, or the benefits, and perhaps even the legitimacy, of other approaches. Or they may devalue other methodologies by, for example, defining their own as the gold standard for informing instructional practice (e.g., National Reading Panel, 2000). Their commitment is to valuing and using a methodology compatible with their worldview, not in adopting methods and approaches that accommodate the complexities of instructional practice and that directly inform day-to-day practice. So one main reason that formative and design experiments are needed is that they represent an approach grounded in making a difference in the real world, not in exercising methodological purity or in privileging one methodology over another.

We are by no means the first to suggest that there are limitations associated with the currently dominant paradigms for conducting education research. For example, Lagemann (2000) has argued that what she characterizes as the troubled history of education research is a result of researchers seeking legitimacy by adopting the methods and perspectives of the hard sciences, instead of seeking methods that are suited specifically to the goals of education. Likewise, Labaree (1998) argued that education research has produced a "lesser form of knowledge" (p. 4) that is more rural (diverse landscapes of shallow, less integrated knowledge) than urban (skyscrapers of deep, integrated knowledge). Dillon and colleagues (2000) pointed out that literacy researchers are often too consumed by methodological and philosophical debates, and they challenged researchers to shift their focus to investigating how we bring about desirable outcomes in literacy instruction.

Formative and design experiments represent a category of research that addresses each of these concerns. First, they represent an approach to research that has arisen from within the field of education and that is aimed specifically at achieving the goals of education. That approach to research is uniquely suited to the kind of knowledge educators seek and need to improve instruction. The emerging conceptual and methodological frameworks, and standards of rigor, for conducting formative and design experiments, as outlined later in Chapter 2, have arisen in the context of efforts to conduct research that has strong potential to provide specific guidance to educators and to create theory and models useful to them. Second, formative and design experiments invite sustained, in-depth research activity aimed at investigating instructional interventions within and across authentic contexts. They offer potential to build the skyscrapers of knowledge that Labaree (1998) indicated are characteristic of more mature fields of endeavor. Third, as we discuss in more detail in the following section, formative and design experiments avoid the distracting philosophical questions and arguments associated with methodological debates.

More recently and more specifically among literacy researchers, Pressley, Graham, and Harris (2006) evaluated the state of education intervention research focusing on literacy research and found it currently inadequate. Their conclusions and recommendations, which we believe are particularly relevant to answering the question posed in this section, included the need for more of the following in relation to intervention research: (1) multiple theoretical perspectives, (2) attention to process variables that explain how and why interventions work or don't work, (3) attention to "the rich array of outcomes and relationships that might be impacted by the intervention" (p. 6), (4) methodologies that accommodate the multiple interacting factors that determine success or lack of success in various environments, (5) more generalizable understandings from cross-case studies using qualitative methods, (6) intensive multiyear studies to produce data relevant to policy makers, and (7) efforts to better communicate results in a form useful to practitioners. Formative and design experiments address these needs.

Nonetheless, perhaps the greatest need met and the greatest usefulness provided by formative and design experiments is, as we highlighted in the introduction to this chapter, that they insert into the research landscape the perspective of engineering science to guide gathering and analyzing data toward the application, refinement, and generation of pedagogical theory in real classrooms. As Robert Ebel (1982) stated many years ago in his presidential address to the American Educational Research Association, "[Education] is not in need of research to find out *how* it works. It is in need of creative invention to *make* it work better" (p. 18, emphasis in original). Formative and design experiments respond to that challenge. They also respond to Pogrow's (1996) observation:

> The feeling is widespread in the [research/academic/reform] community that its responsibility is to produce general theory and that it is up to practitioners to figure out how to apply that theory. . . . It is far more difficult to figure out how to implement theory than it is to generate it. (p. 658)

And, speaking to literacy researchers, Harste (1993; see also Duffy, 1994; Otto, 1992) argued that "the development of a research methodology that truly fits the intent of our discipline [is] one of the great unfinished agenda items of our profession" (p. 358). If formative and design experiments are not the final response to that challenge, they are certainly a step in the right direction.

1.3. What Kind of Knowledge Do Formative and Design Experiments Lay Claim to Creating and on What Basis Is that Claim Made?

Given the contemporary literature about research methodology in education, the question posed in this section is perhaps necessary. A concern about how different research methodologies produce different types of knowledge based on different assumptions about reality is the legacy of the now largely dormant debates between quantitative and qualitative researchers during the 1990s and to a general shift toward postmodern views in academia. Unfortunately, in our view, many education and literacy researchers today continue to judge alternative research methodologies not primarily on whether a particular methodology can generate data that inform educators in useful and productive ways but on what view of knowledge and reality a particular methodology is based. We agree with Dillon and colleagues (2000) that a preoccupation with such philosophical issues has not served the field of literacy well. Nonetheless, we can imagine a doctoral student conducting a formative or design experiment having a committee member who expects the student to articulate how this approach to research fits into these philosophical questions, and we offer a response here.

In regard to defining reality (ontology) and how it can be known (epistemology), we believe that pragmatism provides an appropriate and useful philosophical basis for formative and design experiments and indeed for all education research. Pragmatism is appealing not only because it is well matched to the rationale and perspectives associated with formative and design experiments, but because John Dewey, one of the icons of American education, was also a major promoter of that philosophy. It is beyond the scope of this book to discuss fully all the dimensions of pragmatism in relation to issues of research methodology. (See Johnson & Onwuegbuzie, 2004, for an excellent summary of the basic tenets of pragmatism in relation to education research and Maxey, 2003, for a brief summary of the history of pragmatism in relation to social science research.) However, we highlight here a few of its tenets in relation to formative and design experiments.

Cherryholmes (1992), in his comparison of pragmatism and scientific realism, provided a succinct summary of how the philosophy of pragmatism can be applied to education research:

> Research in a pragmatic tradition . . . seeks to clarify meanings and look to consequences. For pragmatists, values and visions of human action and interaction precede a search for descriptions, theories, explanations, and narratives. Pragmatic research is driven by anticipated consequences. Pragmatic choices about what to research and

> how to go about it are conditioned by where we want to go in the broadest of senses. Values, aesthetics, politics, and social and normative preference are integral to pragmatic research, its interpretation, and utilization. (p. 13)

To pragmatists, determining what works in accomplishing consensually valued goals is as far as we can go to pinning down reality. Pragmatists opt out of the deeper, and ultimately unanswerable, question of what reality is and how we can know it. They focus exclusively on choosing among alternatives that move us closer to our goals. Philosophical issues that do not pertain to our goals and the choices we must make to achieve them are of little importance. And, as highlighted in the quote from Cherryholmes, debates about "values, aesthetics, politics, and social and normative preference" take precedence over debates about reality. Once we agree about what is valued and important, reality becomes the process and means for getting there.

The need to decide what we value introduces another important tenet of pragmatism: a commitment to democratic ideals in establishing worthwhile goals and the means to achieve them. Further, pragmatism is democratically oriented to tolerating a variety of beliefs, as long as they are based in and consistent with furthering human well-being (see Hostetler, 2005). Thus, from the perspective of pragmatism, the knowledge that formative and design experiments generate is how to get from a current less satisfactory condition to a subsequent more satisfactory condition. Less and more satisfactory are defined in terms of democratic dialogue among all stakeholders and grounded in a commitment to human well-being. Formative and design experiments are more likely to focus on such questions because they identify explicit goals for instruction and typically provide an explicit rationale for their relevance and importance.

Wagner (1993), although he was not writing explicitly as a pragmatist, offered a perspective on truth that is consistent with pragmatism and thus with an epistemological stance that can support formative and design experiments. He argued that educational researchers should focus not on seeking truth but on reducing ignorance, in part because we know a lot more about the latter and because recognizing ignorance connects us more directly to well-defined problems and issues. Put another way, education researchers should ask not how much closer their work takes them to the truth but how far beyond ignorance their work moves the field, particularly in terms of what might be accomplished in schools and classrooms. For example, instead of doing research aimed at finding the one truly best way to teach phonics, we might instead approach our research as incremental steps toward reducing our ignorance about when to teach or not to teach phonics, knowing when to use one approach as opposed to another, and grasping which factors enhance or undermine promising, theoretically grounded instructional activities.

We believe formative and design experiments are also consistent with pragmatism's view of theory, experimentation, and causality. For example, to pragmatists, theories must do demonstrable work. As Cherryholmes (1992) has stated, "Pragmatists choose some explanations or theories or stories and dismiss others when the former produce results they desire better than the latter. . . . It is only by acting on our beliefs [and theories] and observing the consequences that we would know whether our beliefs worked" (p. 15). Given this view of theory, experimentation takes on a different, broader meaning than it does in conventional science, and indeed it must to accommodate the considerable variation that is characteristic of classrooms and schools and that is nearly impossible to subject to careful control. For example, we believe that experimentation in pragmatic research is consistent with Schön's (1987) views of reflection-in-action. He identified three types of experimentation often employed by the reflective practitioner: (1) *exploratory,* actions taken simply to see what follows; (2) *move-testing,* deliberate actions to determine if those actions do or do not produce intended results; and (3) *hypothesis testing,* actions intended to determine whether one hypothesis works better than another. All three may be used pragmatically in formative and design experiments, whereas the latter is the only one typically employed in conventional scientific experiments.

Likewise, most pragmatists "give up the idea that we will ever be able to pin down 'underlying causal entities'" (Cherryholmes, 1992, p. 15). In short, causes are less relevant than consequences. Seeking discrete, overarching causes is less reasonable in complex environments shaped by a complex array of interacting variables. More important than a search for ultimate causes and effects (immutable laws) to guide teaching and learning in classrooms may be the local (*mid-level theory* according to Lehrer & Schauble, 2004, and *humble theory* according to Cobb et al., 2003a) theories that researchers using formative and design experiments are inclined to seek and that may be more useful to practitioners. To pragmatists, causality built on understanding and interpreting relations between phenomena is transformed into considering the various dimensions of "making use of" or "coping with" (Rorty, 1991), which we believe is much more appropriate than seeking grand theories of causation that are based on statistical probabilities and that devalue complex contextual variations.

1.4. Can the Results of Formative and Design Experiments Be Generalized?

A doctoral student proposing or defending a dissertation using a formative or design experiment might also be asked to comment on the extent to which findings from this approach may generalize beyond a single context or set of contexts. Part of the answer, we believe, is framing the issue of generalization differently; that is, asking: Generalization for whom and for what purposes? Generalization may be defined and valued differently by researchers, policy makers, and teachers. For example, a generalization derived from a statistical comparisons of instructional program X and Y, uncluttered by a consideration of the complex factors that may have profound effects on implementation, may be useful to a policy maker who must set policy across a diverse range of contexts. Likewise, it may be useful to a researcher trying to support or develop a general theory. But how useful is the same generalization to a teacher looking for guidance in implementing an intervention with a particular group of students in a particular set of circumstances? In that case, a different view of generalization may be more appropriate. Or, as Cronbach (1975) stated many years ago, "when we give proper weight to local conditions, any generalization is a working hypothesis, not a conclusion" (p. 125).

We believe formative and design experiments have much potential for providing generalizations that are useful to teachers and that may guard against putting too much faith in what might be argued to be the overzealous generalizations to which policy makers and researchers are sometimes prone. For example, Hoadley (2004) argued that to produce useful inferences, rigorous research must have *systemic validity*, which means a close alignment among theories, the interventions investigated, and the type of instruction used to implement those interventions. As he stated, "the whole research endeavor must not only create a fair test of the theories, but those theories must be communicated in a way that is true to the inferences used to prove them" (p. 204). In other words, generalizations without this close alignment are abstract, potentially misleading, or at least less useful. Hoadley also argued that the downside of this view is that strong generalizations in a conventional sense across diverse contexts is difficult to achieve "until many designs and enactments are allowed to occur and to be studied formally. The upside is that the knowledge generated is applicable from the very beginning" (p. 211).

We also agree with Bannan-Ritland (2003) that for formative and design experiments, generalizations take on a different meaning and emphasis when compared to narrower views associated with scientific experimentation. She stated:

> [My view of design research] considers multiple . . . data streams with the primary goal being not global warranted propositions, but the creation of products, artifacts, or processes that leverage learning and teaching by making insights usable, actionable, and adoptable. The question becomes not simply one of warrant abstractly, but warrant for whom and for what purposes. (p. 24)

We would add, "Under what circumstances?"

Firestone (1993) provided a general methodological argument that supports these views of generalization. He pointed out that in addition to generalization based on extrapolation from a sample to a population there are at least two other categories for generalizing from data: (1) analytic generalization or extrapolation using theory and (2) case-to-case translation. In the first category, a researcher "makes predictions, and then confirms [or presumably disconfirms] those predictions"; further, "Sometimes analytic generalization attempts to show that a theory holds broadly across a wide variety of circumstances, but sometimes it identifies the scope of a theory—that is, *the conditions under which it applies*" (p. 17, emphasis added). Confirming or disconfirming pedagogical theory through educational interventions that are fundamentally theoretical artifacts is an essential characteristic of formative and design experiments as an approach to research.

Firestone also suggested that analytic generalization is better suited to theories that are narrower in scope and more practice based (e.g., classroom management theories) rather than broader and more abstract (e.g., a theory of cognitive dissonance). That view is echoed in the work of prominent researchers who have written about and used design experiments. For example, Cobb and colleagues (2003a) stated that humble theory tied to particulars is the appropriate theory to guide design experiments. Likewise, Leher and Schauble (2004) refer to theory in their design experiment as

> "mid-level" [theory] because it is more general than a particular set of actions taken in the specific context of investigation, yet its implications for learning are better instantiated (and thus more testable) than those of the more familiar Theories [capitalization in original] of education and psychology. (p. 638)

Case-to-case transfer as a form of generalization also fits well with formative and design experiments, particularly in relation to their value for informing practice. Firestone (1993) described this form of generalization as occurring "whenever a person in one setting considers adopting a program or idea from another one" (p. 17). Put simply, generalization might be achieved in a formative or design experiment when an educator finds the data provided about a studied intervention to be particularly useful to his or her practice. Firestone pointed out that such case-to-case transfer is well developed in the fields of law, medicine, and clinical psychology. However, he emphasized, this view of generalization requires thick descriptions and rigorous data analysis, as we describe in Chapter 2.

Finally, generalizations from formative and design experiments can be achieved through replication. The purpose of replication within the paradigm of conventional scientific experimentation, in the rare instances that it is actually done, is to increase reliability by subjecting hypotheses to falsification. That is, do findings in a particular study stand up to precise replication with another sample in the same population? However, replication plays a different role in creating the type of generalization formative and design experiments might best achieve. When formative and design experiments are replicated across diverse instructional contexts, they may reveal generalizations and theoretical findings that transcend the complex variability across classrooms and the teachers and students that inhabit them. Thus, generalizations in scientific experiments treat variability as a collection of random factors. In formative and design experiments, generalizations are derived from a careful consideration of that variability.

Generalization of data is both a conceptual and a methodological issue, which makes a fitting bridge to Chapter 2. Here we have examined the broad conceptual issues related to defining and characterizing formative and design experiments, particularly in comparison to more established and widely used methodologies in education research. In Chapter 2 we look more specifically at the methods for planning, conducting, and reporting formative and design experiments.

What Are the Methods of Formative and Design Experiments?

Several issues cloud an answer to this overarching question for Chapter 2 and explain why the question cannot be answered as clearly and concisely as it might be for more established approaches to education research. Researchers who are interested in formative and design experiments have been attracted by the conceptual power of this approach; however, they have struggled to precisely define its methodological parameters. Consequently, there are no books or manuals providing explicit guidance on widely agreed-upon methods or specific standards of methodological rigor. In fact, much of the literature about this approach is aimed at aligning its conceptual and methodological dimensions (e.g., Hoadley, 2004) or offering frameworks for conducting and reporting studies. Further, discussions of its limitations mention its lack of methodological clarity (e.g., Dede, 2004).

However, as we pointed out in Chapter 1, to some extent the purpose and goals of formative and design experiments suggest an inherent flexibility in methods, which may mean some inevitable ambiguity. That is, for researchers who conduct formative and design experiments, the methods they employ always serve the central goal of putting theory to work in a way that simultaneously informs practice and refines or generates useful theory grounded in practice. The validity and rigor of their methods are established by creating this alignment between theory and practice. As Hoadley (2004) stated, "In design-based research, the process of forcing the same people to engage the theory, the implementation of interventions, and the measurement of outcomes encourages a greater degree of methodological alignment" (p. 205). Just as an engineer or inventor may draw on different tools and approaches in creating a workable product and understanding the underlying processes that make it work, researchers conducting formative or design experiments may draw on unique configurations of methods for data collection and analysis in carrying out their work in classrooms (see Eisenhart & Borko, 1993). They may employ a variety of quantitative and qualitative methodologies, often holding themselves accountable to the methodological guidelines and standards of rigor associated with those methodologies, including mixed methodologies.

Yet it is not simply a matter of arguing that the methodological guidelines and standards associated with the more conventional methodologies applied in the conceptual frame of formative and design experiments can be adopted wholesale by those using this approach. As Schoenfeld (2006) argued:

> Conducting a high-quality design experiment that produces well-warranted research findings . . . is extremely difficult both in terms of the design effort and the research effort. Making the case for research findings in a design experiment often calls for a combination of planning and opportunism . . . some of the most powerful findings will be serendipitous, and the data to support them will be marshaled *post hoc*. Conducting such work rigorously demands very high standards, and the field is still sorting out how to grapple with such issues (p. 202).

Thus, researchers who conduct formative and design experiments cannot excuse themselves from specifying methodological guidelines and standards of rigor that distinguish between weak and strong reasons for conclusions and findings, and thus they must contend with trustworthiness of data and credibility of assertions. Nonetheless, because the goals of formative and design experiments are distinctly different from those of other approaches to education research, they will be guided by different methods and different forms of justification (Gravemeijer & Cobb, 2006).

Complicating the methodological picture is that the goals in a particular investigation are multilayered, including, for example, data that (1) characterize the school and classroom context specifically in relation to the intervention, (2) guide modifications to the intervention in the local environment, and (3) speak to the larger theoretical issues and potential application to other environments (see Joseph, 2004). There may be different guidelines and standards that come into play in addressing each of these subgoals, but there also need to be broader guidelines and standards that merge these purposes and goals into a coherent whole. We do not claim to present here the definitive methodological guidelines and standards for conducting and evaluating the rigor of formative and design experiments, and we certainly do not claim to have found the methodological coherence that continues to be sought. However, drawing on the literature and our own work, we aim here to provide some guidelines, standards, and frameworks that we hope will guide researchers interested in using this approach and in evaluating the methodological legitimacy and rigor of a particular investigation.

2.1. What Types of Data Are Collected?

A quote from Jacob (1992) provides a succinct answer to this question for formative experiments. She stated:

> In . . ."formative experiments" . . . researchers [have] a specific educational goal in mind. They then [modify] the materials or the social organization to bring about the desired goal. The approaches [use] traditional ethnographic methods, such as participant observations and videotaping, to identify problems, to propose possible solutions, and to document before, during, and after change. (p. 322)

Likewise, Collins (1999), writing about design experiments, stated:

> Design experiments ideally are much more like what *Consumer Reports* does when it evaluates the quality of different automobiles. The goal is to look at many different aspects of the design and develop a qualitative and quantitative profile that characterizes the design in practice. (p. 292)

These quotes suggest characteristics of data collection, analysis, and interpretation in formative and design experiments. First, formative and design experiments clearly fall into a category of research that Salomon (1991) characterizes as systemic approaches (i.e., research that treats variables as interdependent and transactional), as opposed to analytic approaches (i.e., research that treats variables as isolable for discrete study). Systemic research seeks to determine "*that which happens* in actuality under normal conditions" (Salomon, 1991, p. 16, emphasis in original). Likewise, systemic research produces rich descriptive theories. Thus, researchers who conduct formative and design experiment must, most fundamentally, acquire data that produce rich explanatory descriptions that link interdependent variables in an authentic educational context to pedagogical outcomes in ways that inform theory.

The central issue of data collection in formative and design experiments is not whether quantitative or qualitative data are gathered (or the philosophical debates often accompanying that distinction) but what data can best generate the systemic understandings that inform theory development in the real world of practice. Nonetheless, systemic approaches, including formative and design experiments, necessitate the use of at least some qualitative data, because they examine a wide array of potentially relevant interacting variables and factors that are difficult to manage using quantitative methods alone. Thus, it is inconceivable that a formative and design experiment could be conducted without qualitative data. However, quantitative data may be quite useful, particularly in establishing a baseline of performance related to a pedagogical goal that a formative or design experiment is aimed at moving toward and likewise in determining whether progress has been made at the conclusion of a study.

For example, in our own work (Reinking & Watkins, 2000) our goal was to increase the amount of independent reading among adolescents using an intervention that involved students in creating multimedia book reviews. To assess the extent to which that goal was achieved, we quantified survey data on independent reading and used a standardized instrument for measuring attitudes about reading. After several months of implementing and fine-tuning the intervention, a process informed by prodigious qualitative data, we readministered the survey, comparing that data to the baseline and also making statistical comparisons to other students who had been using an alternative program for increasing independent reading. Thus, our approach employed both quantitative data used for statistical comparisons aimed at determining the extent to which our goal had been achieved and qualitative data aimed at determining what factors enhanced or inhibited the effectiveness of our intervention. However, quantitative data might also be useful in some cases when implementing an intervention. For example, quantitative data, such as recording the number and type of interactions between teachers and students, might be used to inform instructional moves to refine an intervention aimed at improving the quality of those interactions.

As these examples illustrate, there is a natural marriage between formative and design experiments and the emerging use of mixed methods for collecting and analyzing data in education research (see Chatterji, 2004; Johnson & Onwuegbuzie, 2004; Tashakkori & Teddlie, 1998, 2003). As Eisenhart and Borko (1993) have argued, researchers who work in classrooms may need to have great flexibility and latitude in blending qualitative and quantitative approaches to data collection and analysis if they are to generate findings that are truly integrative, not just additive, and if their findings are to speak coherently to classroom practice. Nonetheless, they also argued that researchers who creatively blend methods must explain and justify their methodological choices, which we believe is also necessary for researchers who conduct formative and design experiments.

Although a variety of qualitative approaches to data collection might be employed within and across various formative and design experiment (e.g., case studies, interviews, discourse analyses), we believe that the approaches categorized as ethnographic research are generally most useful and are likely to be called for most often. Ethnographic approaches are well suited to the ecological perspective that drives formative and design experiments and the examination of how an intervention plays out in the culture of a particular classroom and school. For example, as Purcell-Gates (2004) suggested:

> [An ethnographic approach] calls for research questions, or research foci, that seek to situate the researcher into a cultural landscape for the purpose of exploration and discovery of answers to questions like *why, what is happening, what does it look like, how does it work,* and so on. (p. 95, emphasis in original)

To us, these questions are the very ones that are necessary to address when a pedagogical theory is instantiated by introducing an instructional intervention into a classroom culture. However, unlike the usual application of ethnographic approaches, the goal is not simply a rich description that characterizes a cultural landscape. The data have a much more functional and pragmatic mission. That is, the ethnographic data guide efforts to fully integrate an intervention into a classroom culture for the sake of accomplishing a valued pedagogical goal and for the sake of extending theoretical understandings of what is likely to work or not work in actual practice.

2.2. What Are the Goals of Data Collection?

One approach to defining the methods of formative and design experiments is to focus on the goals of data collection. We offer the following goals, which have guided our own research and which we believe capture major goals of data collection that have been explicit or implicit in the work of others involved in this approach to research.

1. Characterizing the instructional context. We believe that formative and design experiments should typically include the systematic collection of data that provide what is often called a *thick description* of the instructional environment before an intervention is introduced, using ethnographic observational methods and interviews. That is, using ecology as an underlying metaphor of this approach means collecting data that characterize that ecology at the outset of an investigation and tracking changes as the intervention is introduced. These data should answer questions such as: How do teachers view their work in general? What is the relationship between teachers and students? What kind of instructional and social climate does the teacher establish in the classroom? What are the teachers' (and students') views of teaching and learning, particularly in areas related to the proposed intervention? What is the administrative climate of the school? What materials are available and used for instruction? What routines govern the flow of classroom activities? What school rules or routines influence classroom activities? The depth of data gathered, analyzed, and reported may not be equivalent to a rigorous ethnography, but these data and their interpretation should extend beyond a perfunctory description. Such data and analysis may also be useful during the experiment (see subsequent item 5).

2. Establishing baseline performance or conditions prior to introducing the intervention. Data are needed to establish a benchmark against which progress might be measured in relation to accomplishing a pedagogical goal or bringing about desired changes in perspective, practice, or behavior. These data may be quantitative and/or qualitative. In the previously cited example from our own work, the data were primarily quantitative (survey data and a standardized inventory of attitudes toward reading in and out of school); however, these data were supplemented by ethnographic observations such as students' engagement in reading during free time.

3. Identifying factors that enhance and inhibit movement toward a specified pedagogical goal. Specifically, data need to be gathered to identify the factors that speak to an intervention's effectiveness and efficiency in reaching a pedagogical goal and, in many instances, its appeal to all stakeholders (primarily teachers and students, but also perhaps administrators, parents, and so on). We believe that such data are at the heart of formative and design experiments, because they simultaneously inform theory and practice. More immediately, such data provide guidance about what instructional moves and adaptations may be necessary to further the effectiveness, efficiency, and appeal of an instructional intervention. For example, if the intervention was book sharing, a teacher's beliefs about and purpose for reading aloud, the role and perspectives of a teaching assistant, the instructional routines, the number of children participating in a book sharing, the genre of text typically read, and so forth are all factors that might influence the effectiveness of a book reading activity in a preschool classroom. Such data are likely to entail qualitative observations and interviews.

4. Documenting the effects of instructional moves aimed at enhancing the effects of an intervention. This goal is a companion to the previous one. Together they form an iterative, but often fluid, cycle consisting first of determining what factors enhance or inhibit an intervention's effectiveness, which informs adaptations of the intervention or the way it is implemented, and then determining if those adaptations have achieved a desired effect. Instructional moves may be made to capitalize on an enhancing factor or to circumvent or neutralize an inhibiting factor. These moves are made iteratively, drawing on relevant data and evolving theory to determine moves that test hypotheses about what is occurring and how the intervention might be improved within the constraints of a particular classroom. This process may entail short-term microcycles in the context of implementing the intervention in individual classrooms or in longer-term macrocycles across separate implementations of the intervention. Figure 2.1 illustrates this process.

However, in our experience, the vagaries of instructional practice often mean that these cycles are fluid and overlapping, and it is not always easy to isolate the effects of individual instructional moves, many of which are occurring simultaneously. Further, instruction and the effects of an intervention are ongoing. A researcher cannot return the instructional environment to a previous state to determine whether a different course of action might produce different effects. Nonetheless, given this limitation, a researcher's goal is to collect data about the effects of an instructional move as a way of validating or invalidating the interpretations and hypothesis that led to making the move in the first place. That is, if an instructional adaptation produces the desired effects based on data identifying factors that enhance or inhibit effectiveness, the original data and its interpretations gain a measure of validity, as perhaps does the theory that inspired it or that is evolving.

Figure 2.1. A representation of micro- and macrocycles of data collection and analysis in design research

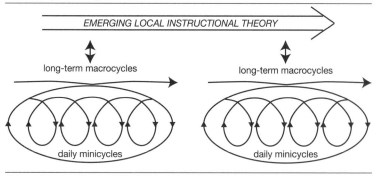

Source: Gravemeijer & Cobb (2006).

To document whether the desired effects have been achieved, quantitative and qualitative data might be useful. For example, consider a situation in which data indicate that an intervention aimed at increasing vocabulary knowledge seems less effective because students have little opportunity to discuss the subtleties of word meanings. A researcher and a teacher then agree to modify the intervention to make room for such discussions. Data validating that move might be quantitative data indicating increases in vocabulary knowledge on an assessment of vocabulary knowledge (e.g., a quiz after the lesson) as well as qualitative data suggesting that students have a greater awareness of or engagement with word meanings during a science lesson. That data could then confirm or disconfirm whether discussion was an operative factor in the intervention's effectiveness and perhaps an important element of an emerging pedagogical theory. However, a quiz, too, becomes an element of the intervention, perhaps with its own effects, which illustrates the complex interactions among instructional moves and the difficulty in isolating instructional factors and moves for study.

5. Identifying and seeking explanations for unanticipated effects and outcomes. Given the complexity of educational contexts and instructional practice, implementing an instructional intervention will invariably produce unanticipated effects and outcomes, some of which may be neither directly related to the intervention's pedagogical goal nor anticipated by whatever theory guides the instructional intervention. Dewey referred to these effects as collateral learning, and they are important for at least two reasons: (1) They suggest modifications to existing theory or the development of new theory, and (2) they suggest further research that might be aimed at accomplishing other goals or testing other theories. In our view, researchers conducting formative and design experiments should take steps to ensure that their data collection, analysis, and interpretation allow for identifying such effects and outcomes. Some of these data may directly inform adaptations and instructional moves, and are thus incorporated into the previous two goals of data collection. Other data may not inform directly how the intervention should be modified, but they may be important to fully understanding the intervention's effects, practically and theoretically, and perhaps to informing future studies. For example, in our own work (Reinking & Watkins, 2000), integrating computer technology into the elementary school language arts curriculum to increase independent reading produced ancillary effects such as increased parental interest and involvement in the classroom and greater attention to the mechanics of writing in developing online book reviews shared with teachers, peers, and parents.

6. Determining the extent to which an intervention has transformed a learning environment. Often, an aim of a formative or design experiment is to positively transform teaching and learning beyond the narrow pedagogical goals of the intervention. In fact, one reason to investigate a particular intervention is that it has potential for changing more fundamentally the ecology of teaching and learning. For example, an intervention may be aimed at increasing students' vocabulary or increasing their ability to read critically, but it may also be thought to have potential to change the way teachers and students attend to and deal with vocabulary or to approach texts critically across the curriculum. Transformations might be considered at different levels, including teachers' orientations, classroom activities, student participation, curriculum, and overall classroom culture. Particularly in those investigations where there is an explicit goal to transform the learning environment, appropriate quantitative and qualitative data need to be gathered, analyzed, and interpreted systematically to determine if such transformations are occurring.

7. Identifying conditions under which an intervention does or does not work well toward developing theory and improving practice. This goal is a distinctly general one, and to some extent it encompasses all of the previous goals. The relevant data, too, are likely to be found among those data gathered to address the previous goals. However, for some researchers, specifically Cobb and his colleagues (Cobb et al., 2003a; Gravemeijer & Cobb, 2006), addressing this goal is the essential phase of data analysis carried out after all the data have been collected and the investigation has been completed. They term this phase a *retrospective analysis* because it takes place post hoc, drawing on field notes, videotapes, interviews, and so forth collected throughout the investigation. This is a meta-analytic phase documenting the history of conjectures that were supported or refuted by the data gathered during the investigation aimed at drawing conclusions, clarifying theory, and offering recommendations. In that sense, it is also closely aligned with reporting findings. In any event, the data that address this goal are at the nexus of the research–practice interface where formative and design experiments uniquely dwell.

8. *Comparing and contrasting the effects of an intervention (or alternative interventions) across diverse contexts.* This goal pertains to the scale of a formative or design experiment. The scale of an investigation has implications for its design and thus for data collection, analysis, and interpretation. Although it may not always be feasible, as with other methodologies, larger-scale studies provide greater opportunity to compare and contrast an intervention's implementation and effects across a broader range of contexts. For example, a funded project might provide the resources enabling a comparison of the effectiveness and ease of implementing an intervention of interest to an alternative intervention in another classroom or a control classroom. Likewise, large-scale projects might allow a team of researchers to compare how the intervention works across several diverse classrooms, perhaps selected purposefully to represent a range of conditions. Data across different sites and conditions can then be compared to determine points of convergence or divergence, which can enhance theory development and case-to-case generalizations (see Section 1.4). Smaller-scale studies in particular may benefit from including a comparison classroom as a control or one that employs an alternative intervention aimed specifically at achieving the overarching pedagogical goal. In such instances, when quantitative data are gathered, statistical comparisons might be made.

2.3 What Are Standards for Determining Methodological Rigor?

This question, too, has not been fully addressed or resolved in the literature, at least beyond the standards of rigor associated with the collection and analysis of data in quantitative, qualitative, or mixed methods approaches in general. But establishing rigor is an important issue if design experiments are to be taken seriously within the community of education researchers. For example, doctoral students who wish to conduct a formative or design experiment must be able to convince members of their dissertation committees that there are standards that can be invoked to establish rigor and to distinguish between a weak and a strong investigation. Although certainly not the final word, we believe the following benchmarks provide a foundation for establishing methodological rigor for formative and design experiments:

1. Conceptual rigor. As Hoadley (2004) argued, the rigor of design research is based fundamentally on a close alignment of theory, research, and practice, what he calls *systemic validity.* Thus, a starting point for establishing the rigor of a formative or design experiment is an explicit articulation of how these three elements are represented and cohere in a particular investigation. Likewise, the investigation must have what Messick (1992) referred to as *consequential validity.* That is, a researcher must articulate how the intervention of interest might make a difference in accomplishing a well-defined and valued pedagogical goal. More specifically, the intervention should include most or all of the defining characteristics discussed in Section 1.1.2: It should be theoretical, goal oriented, intervention centered, adaptive and iterative, transformative, methodologically inclusive, and pragmatic.

2. Attention and openness to multiple factors and to multiple sources of data. A rigorous formative or design experiment is one in which a researcher considers a wide range of factors that may influence the implementation of the intervention and its potential effects. Consequently, rigor also means considering multiple sources of data for systematic analysis in order to reveal those factors. Hostetler (2005) described good educational research as an "intense scrutiny of particulars" (p. 18), which is an especially apt phrase for describing rigorous formative and design experiments. However, that intense scrutiny must bear the tangible fruit of allowing the intervention to become more effective and to be more efficiently implemented.

For example, a literacy researcher investigating an intervention aimed at helping second-language learners become more involved in reading English texts might attend to the type of texts used, students' reactions to them, students' cultural and linguistic backgrounds, teachers' orientations to teaching second-language learners, the social interaction patterns in a classroom, students' motivation to read in their first and second languages, how instruction is scheduled, the physical arrangement of the classroom, and so forth. Some of these factors may be of theoretical importance or identified a priori in relation to the pedagogical goal and assessed formally or informally at specific points during the investigation, perhaps through quantitative measures. Others will emerge during the investigation, but only if a researcher is open to finding them.

In any event, multiple sources of data are necessary to acquire a deep understanding of the intervention and its effects. For example, the researcher may take field notes during classroom observations, interview teachers and students, ask teachers to keep a log of their thoughts and observations, and analyze students' responses to their readings. Flexibility in the data collected and how the data are analyzed is also characteristic of formative and design experiments. Changing conditions during an investigation or emerging findings may suggest that different data are needed or more effective approaches to analysis are warranted. For example, after a month of implementing the intervention aimed at promoting more second-language reading, a teacher, perhaps in response to data provided by the researcher, may decide to enrich the intervention by having students develop PowerPoint presentations related to their reading (e.g., Ivey & Broaddus, 2007). The researcher might logically include these presentations as data and seek an appropriate approach to analyzing them. However, a rigorous report of the investigation will provide an explicit rationale for the initial approach to data collection and analysis and will explain and justify any modifications that were made in response to changing conditions.

In fact, as this latter example illustrates, openness, flexibility, and adaptability in considering multiple factors and multiple sources of data are an essential component of formative and design experiments. In one sense, this approach to research is about looking for and documenting the unexpected. It is an approach that tries to define the critical and complexly interacting factors that impinge on the effectiveness of an intervention and explores how to manage those factors in ways that cannot be readily predicted and that may produce unanticipated effects. Thus, data collection and analysis that embrace openness, flexibility, and adaptability reflect rigor, although that does not obviate the usefulness of a carefully considered plan for data collection at the outset of an investigation.

3. *Triangulation.* According to Creswell (2002), triangulation "is the process of corroborating evidence from different individuals, . . . types of data, . . . or methods of data collection" (p. 280). Tashakkori and Teddlie (1998) added the notion of "theoretical triangulation" (p. 41), whereby different theoretical positions converge to explain data and support conclusions. We believe that all of these aspects of triangulation are consistent with the intent of formative and design experiments and may contribute to establishing the rigor of an investigation using this approach. That is, data collection and analysis that produce convergent evidence from multiple sources through multiple methods produce findings, interpretations, and recommendations that are more trustworthy and convincing, and thus more rigorous. Thus, triangulation is a natural extension of the previous section specifying the importance of attending to multiple sources of data and of taking a flexible stance toward the methods used to collect and analyze data.

For example, consider a study investigating an intervention aimed at increasing beginning readers' use of analogous key words on a word wall to decode unfamiliar written words (e.g., decoding *rip* by comparing it to the key word *tip* on the word wall). A researcher might note while observing lessons that children seem more engaged when the words come from their free reading than from a text the teacher selected. In a debriefing after the lesson, the teacher without prompting makes a similar observation. Subsequent lessons, perhaps using student-selected or teacher-selected texts, are compared, perhaps followed with a focus group discussion with students or a simple survey to discover what they liked or disliked about each lesson. On a broader theoretical level a retrospective analysis of data across the entire investigation might suggest that children employ word analogies to assist in decoding unfamiliar words spontaneously not when they have internalized perfectly all of the key words but when they have encouragement and repeated opportunities to use that approach in relation to texts they find interesting and meaningful. A rigorous formative or design experiment reaching that conclusion would provide supporting data from diverse sources of data using diverse methods.

4. *Adequate time for research.* To be considered rigorous, a formative or design experiment must be conducted for a sufficient time to permit an in-depth analysis of the environment. There must also be sufficient time to explore the effects of an instructional intervention, including many opportunities to adapt it in response to incoming data. Using the metaphors we introduced in Chapter 1, adequate time is needed to determine the ecology of the classroom and to engineer achievement of a pedagogical goal within that ecology. Adequate time is also needed to test and, if necessary, refine theoretical understandings.

Laying the groundwork for an investigation may also require considerable time. For example, recruiting teachers who are open to and comfortable with working closely with a researcher to implement an intervention with a goal to which they are mutually committed, explaining the intervention and its rationale, working through a variety of logistical issues (scheduling instruction, obtaining necessary materials, etc.), and obtaining necessary approvals and permissions can all require even more time than is necessary for other approaches to classroom research. However, that process may be streamlined when a researcher has established an ongoing relationship with a teacher, school, or district. We discuss establishing such a relationship further in Section 2.5.1.

As with other methodologies, there are not specific guidelines for determining adequate time for conducting a rigorous formative or design experiment. However, we believe a rigorous study will typically involve several months of data collection. The complexity of the intervention and the logistical challenges to implementing it play a role in determining what is adequate time. For example, in our experience, interventions involving digital technologies may require more time because they typically entail acquainting teachers and students with new applications, because there are typically logistical challenges related to using new hardware or software, because computer-based materials often need debugging, and because adaptations of the computer-based materials can require reprogramming. Other factors that affect a determination of adequate time include the number of researchers and sites involved in a project, how often the intervention is employed in a classroom (e.g., every day vs. once a week), how often researchers can be on site while teachers and students are engaged in the intervention, and so forth.

5. Interdisciplinary perspectives and use of multiple theories. Another benchmark in determining the rigor of a formative and design experiments is the degree to which it embraces interdisciplinary perspectives and multiple theoretical explanations. Researchers who gravitate toward formative and design experiment are not necessarily trying to find evidence confirming or disconfirming a single, narrowly defined theory, in part because a single theory is unlikely to accommodate all the factors and sources of variability that affect the implementation of the intervention and its effects. Many broad theoretical perspectives may guide implementation and interpretations, leading perhaps to more specific local, humble (Gravemeijer & Cobb, 2006) pedagogical theories or what McKenney and colleagues (2006) referred to as principles of enactment. Considering a wide range of relevant theories is accomplished ideally by assembling interdisciplinary teams, although that is rarely feasible without substantial funding. However, doing so risks diluting the close professional relationship between a researcher and a teacher that we believe is essential in this approach. Indeed, conducting research with an interdisciplinary team was Ann Brown's (1992) original conception of design experiments (see also Eisenhart & Borko, 1993). Nonetheless, we do not believe formative and design experiments necessarily need to involve a team of interdisciplinary researchers in order to be rigorous. However, when conducted by an individual researcher, formative and design experiments are likely to be more rigorous when the researcher is not wedded to one perspective and has a broad interdisciplinary knowledge of potentially relevant theoretical and pedagogical perspectives. By interdisciplinary, we mean both in a broad sense, such as the distinction between cognitive psychology and policy studies, and in a narrower sense, such as different theories of motivation and how those theories might inform instruction.

6. Selection of an appropriate research site. Another benchmark of rigor in conducting formative and design experiments is careful selection of a research site (or sites) and articulation of how and why a site was selected. For example, in survey research a sample of convenience is typically considered a weaker approach than systematic procedures that result in a sample that represents a larger population. On the other hand, as is the case for other methodologies, there are only broad guidelines that might be invoked, and inevitably researchers will likely need to make compromises in selecting a research site.

Nonetheless, selecting a research site, most often a classroom or classrooms in a particular school or district, may be particularly important in formative and design experiments. Lehrer and Schauble (2004) highlighted one consideration when they stated, "in the current study, our interest was not in what typically occurs but in what can occur *under good, but not highly unusual, instructional circumstances*" (p. 640, emphasis added). In other words, other things being equal, a rigorous (and more widely useful) formative or design experiment will not be conducted in schools and classrooms where odds of successful implementation or catastrophic failure of an intervention are unusually high. Likewise, it is probably not wise to select a site where there are many indications that a pedagogical goal of interest has already been achieved or is unproblematic. A good site might be one where initial conditions suggest that the intervention's success will face some barriers and challenges but where conditions are not so overwhelmingly challenging as to doom the intervention to failure.

Of course, these conditions are not always transparent at the stage of selecting the site for research. In fact, we are familiar with some researchers conducting a formative experiment who have been led to withdraw from a site after it became clear that it was fruitless to continue (e.g., a teacher reneging on commitments to the project), which required considerable tact on their part. On the other hand, some have sought out sites or continued to collect data in circumstances that were much less than ideal, realizing that the pedagogical goal was unlikely to be achieved in a particular environment but also realizing that documenting the reasons for failure might produce useful findings and conclusions. On the other hand, as Brown (1992) observed, "the classroom [for research] must function smoothly as a learning environment before we can study anything other than the myriad possible ways that things can go wrong" (p. 141). Thus, other things being equal, a middle ground between an ideal and a distinctly less-than-ideal existing instructional environment might be the best course.

One way around this dilemma is again likely to be an option only with large-scale funded studies. That is, sites can be selected purposefully based on a preliminary assessment to determine the likelihood that the intervention can be implemented easily and successfully. For example, if the intervention involves computer technologies, a range of classrooms having ideal or less-than-ideal resources and circumstances in that regard might be purposefully selected for the sake of comparison. Likewise, schools might be selected on the basis of their commitment to the project and its goals. In that regard we believe the ideal is to locate schools and teachers who are committed and open to working on the project but who are not so enthusiastic that they are willing to go to heroic lengths to make the intervention work.

7. Skepticism, not romanticism or advocacy. It is natural for researchers to favor evidence that is consistent with their pet theories and to interpret data in ways supporting an innovative approach or intervention that they believe holds promise. Or they may have an inclination to interpret their data to conform to romanticized views of education and classroom practice. Researchers who use formative and design experiments are no less susceptible to such tendencies, but it is particularly important that they resist such tendencies in order to conduct rigorous research. As Brown (1992) stated when discussing how not to conduct design experiments, "there is a tendency to romanticize research of this nature and rest claims of success on a few engaging anecdotes or particularly exciting transcripts" (p. 173).

To an extent beyond researchers using other approaches, researchers who use formative and design experiments must not initiate a research project convinced that the intervention they wish to study will certainly produce the desired results, at least without significant modification in its implementation. Failure is always a possibility, but one from which important insights can emerge. They must have a strong commitment to discovering the flaws, weaknesses, and limitations of an intervention and the inadequacy of theories underlying its use. That posture is essential for maintaining rigor and ultimately the credibility of findings. The complex realities of diverse classrooms must be seen as a testing ground for improvement, not obstacles to ignore, play down, or simply work around to maintain a researcher's preconceived notion of how the intervention *should* be implemented. Thus, an investigation that does not convincingly employ methods conducive to discovering the pitfalls of theory in practice, that seems to overlook difficulties in implementing an intervention, or that seems intent on protecting a theoretical view is suspect of lacking appropriate rigor. As Hoadley (2004) stated, for a researcher who conducts design-based research, "the treatments' fidelity to theory is initially, and sometimes continually, suspect" (p. 204). Interestingly, one dimension of this benchmark in our experience is convincing teachers that we are not going to be disappointed with the intervention or with them if the intervention is not easily implemented or perfectly successful. However, once they (and we) let go of such expectations and feelings, we have found it to be decidedly liberating to our own professional lives as researchers and facilitative of positive professional relationships with the teachers with whom we have worked. Once one understands and accepts the perspectives underlying formative and design experiments, it is much easier to let the data speak and to put aside any disappointment that things are not progressing or producing results as planned or as anticipated. It also has the potential to break the not uncommon and depressing cycle of excitement and failure associated with other approaches to investigating innovative instructional interventions in classrooms—a cycle Brown (1992) identifies as "exhilaration, followed by scientific credibility, followed by disappointment and blame" (p. 172, see also Reinking & Pickle, 1993). On a more professionally self-serving level, that stance means that every investigation rigorously conducted is potentially publishable, not just those that produce statistically significant results or results that reside within a narrow theoretical frame.

2.4. What Methodological Frameworks Might Be Used to Conceptualize, Plan, Conduct, and Report Formative and Design Experiments?

There is no single, agreed-upon methodological framework for conceptualizing, planning, conducting, and reporting formative and design experiments. Not surprisingly, the frameworks that we have located in the literature reflect to some extent the diverse disciplinary, theoretical, and methodological backgrounds of the researchers who have become interested in formative and design experiments. In this section we present several of those frameworks, beginning with the foundational work by two of the first researchers to refer to their work as a formative or design experiment, followed by several frameworks that are more recent and more explicit.

2.4.1. Foundational frameworks

Considering frameworks for formative and design experiments must begin with the work of Ann Brown, who was the first researcher to articulate the parameters of this approach to research. Figure 2.2 is reproduced from her seminal 1992 article outlining her conception of design experiments. It represents the first conceptual framework for defining the features of design experiments and implicitly what might or ought to be included in the methods used to conduct one. For example, it suggests that an explicit theory should guide "engineering a working environment" and that task should reciprocally inform theory, although precisely how that reciprocity might be achieved is not explicit in her work.

Elsewhere, she (Brown & Campione, 1996) indicated that her work was guided by what she termed *first principles,* which in her work included the following assumptions: (1) learning is social, (2) metacognition (reflective knowledge about one's knowledge and strategies to enhance it) is fundamental to learning, and (3) individual differences are paramount to learning. These first principles guided her work in designing an intervention that was workable in classrooms for enhancing reading comprehension. Creating such first principles is one way researchers could explicitly state the theory guiding their initial work in classrooms, and thus it might be a basic organizing scheme for conceptualizing, conducting, and reporting their investigation formative.

Likewise, Brown identified some elements of input that should be attended to when conducting a design experiment: classroom ethos, teacher/student as researcher, curriculum, and technology. However, her "etc." in Figure 2.2 leaves room to speculate about what other categories of factors might be considered. Nonetheless, this lack of specificity is put into perspective by Lagemann's (2000) observation that "Brown's simultaneous concern with the curriculum, pedagogy, and assessment . . . differed significantly from older styles of research, which focused on components of the educational process separately" (p. 225). As Brown (1992) herself stated:

Aspects [of classrooms] that are often treated independently, such as teacher training, curriculum selection, testing, and so forth actually form part of a systematic whole. Just as it is impossible to change one aspect of the system without creating perturbations in others, so too it is difficult to study any one aspect independently from the whole operating system. (p. 143)

This systemic perspective was a radical departure from most conventional education research at the time and clearly had methodological implications that were consistent with the interest in qualitative approaches to research emerging at the same time as her work.

Another important methodological perspective that Brown (1992) integrated into her work was that "an effective intervention should be able to migrate from our experimental classroom to average classrooms operated by and for average students and teachers, supported by realistic technological and personal support" (p. 143). The methodological mandate suggested by that view is the importance of selecting appropriate research sites, as discussed in the previous section. It also suggested, as does the lower right oval in Figure 2.2, that dissemination must be rooted in communicating results and findings in ways that are understandable and useful to practitioners.

Figure 2.2. Ann Brown's design experiment

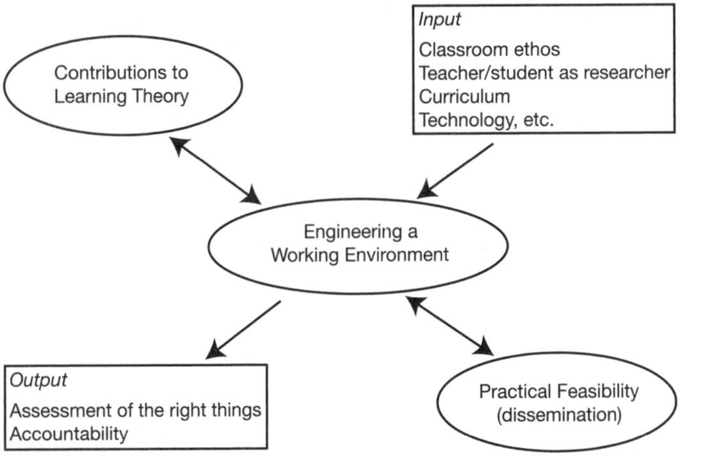

Source: Brown, A. L. (1992).

Just as Brown provided the methodological foundations of design experiments, Newman (1990, 1992) arguably did so for formative experiments. To our knowledge, his 1990 article in *Educational Researcher* was the first peer-reviewed publication reporting empirical work referred to as a formative experiment. In that article he laid out his conception of this approach and reported how he used it to study the effect of a computer-based application on the organizational environment of the classroom. His conceptualization was influenced by his grounding in social psychology, particularly his Vygotskian perspective, and by his interest in developing computer-based applications with the potential not only to enhance learning but also to be a catalyst for transforming educational environments, which he saw as essentially social worlds.

His perspective and the research it inspired were unique for the time, particularly in the realm of research on how computers might enhance teaching and learning. That is, his focus was not only on whether the computer (or any intervention) could produce learning, but also on the interaction between a computer-based intervention and the educational environment. As he stated, "The technology is treated not as the cause of change but as something that can be used, by the school as well as the researcher, to support changes" (Newman, 1990, p. 12). He asked new questions, such as "How does the technology get used or understood differently from the original assumptions of the designers? How does the technology present new interpretations of ways of approaching the work not initially available in the environment?" (Newman, 1992, p. 64).

Pedagogical theory and pedagogical goals also figure prominently in Newman's conceptualization of formative experiments. Although in his 1990 publication he focused mostly on the theoretical foundations for formative experiments as an approach to conducting research, his research was based on the pedagogical theory that students should use computers like scientists do, and his pedagogical goal was to use technology to facilitate an increase in collaborative work among students engaged in science content. More broadly, he stated:

> In a formative experiment, the researcher sets a pedagogical goal and finds out what it takes in terms of materials, organization, or changes in the technology to reach that goal. Instead of rigidly con-

trolling the treatments and observing differences in the outcome, as in a conventional experiment, formative experiments aim at a particular outcome and observe the process by which the goal is achieved. (1990, p. 10)

Thus, Brown's and Newman's early work laid the foundation for more explicit methodological frameworks by focusing on the interplay between the intervention and the educational environment and by viewing an intervention as a means of accomplishing an explicit pedagogical goal and transforming the environment. Likewise, these early frameworks emphasized investigating how the social nature of the educational environment would affect the intervention and how it could be implemented successfully. Newman in particular also saw pedagogical theory as a central component in implementing the intervention. Together these two researchers and their colleagues introduced themes that recur in the later, more explicit methodological frameworks to which we now turn.

2.4.2. Explicit frameworks

Several researchers interested in formative and design experiments have offered more explicit frameworks to systematize the conceptualization, conduct, and reporting of investigations using that approach. Given the methodological inclusiveness and flexibility of formative and design experiments and the varying conceptual emphasis among researchers who have used this approach to research, it is not surprising that distinctly different frameworks have emerged. It remains to be seen whether any one framework will come to dominate or—more likely—whether several frameworks will come to be recognized as legitimate and useful, depending on a researcher's orientation and purposes.

In the remainder of this section, we highlight several frameworks that have been explicated in the literature. We believe they illustrate the diversity of emphases among researchers who have attempted to better define methodologically what formative and design experiments are, what they can accomplish, and how they might be conceptualized and conducted. Each contributes potentially important methodological perspectives and possibilities, and each might be considered as a possible framework for conducting a formative or design experiment.

Reigeluth and Frick (1999). The framework offered by these authors reflects their background in the field of instructional design. Thus, their focus is more on testing and generating theories that might be useful for designing instruction and less on documenting nuances in a specific context. To them, the most basic element of design theory is *"preferability:* the extent to which a method is better than other known methods for attaining the desired outcome" (p. 634). However, preferability has three distinct dimensions: (1) effectiveness, or the degree to which a design theory leads to the accomplishment of a goal; (2) efficiency, or a comparison of effectiveness and cost in time, energy, money, and so forth; and (3) appeal, or "how enjoyable the resulting designs are for the people associated with them" (p. 635). These dimensions alone provide a basic methodological framework for gathering data in a formative or design experiment, and they go notably beyond most conventional experiments investigating interventions, which frequently examine effectiveness in terms of measurable achievement.

For example, using this framework, a literacy researcher conducting a formative experiment investigating how digital versions of popular children's books might be implemented to increase interest in reading would also gather data indicating whether they are appealing not only to students but also to the teacher. Further, the researcher might compare any positive benefits of the digital intervention to the benefits of a less expensive and logistically more manageable activity involving printed materials.

However, as indicated in their taxonomy, reproduced in Figure 2.3, they offer a more explicit framework that might be useful if a researcher is intent on testing theory. Two dimensions are crossed in the taxonomy: (1) whether the theory exists or is new and (2) whether a researcher attempts to implement an intervention designed to test the theory, to determine if the theory is operating by conducting an analysis during an existing case, or if the theory can be found in an analysis after an intervention has occurred. We cannot envision the latter case (i.e., the third row in Figure 2.3), and we are not sure that such cases can legitimately be included as a category of formative and design experiments. However, the first two cases seem clearly aligned with formative and design experiments, and the authors offer the following six methodological steps in implementing those cases (p. 638):

Figure 2.3. Taxonomy of "formative research" studies

	For Existing Theory	For New Theory
Designed Case	Designed case for an existing theory	Designed case for a new theory
In Vivo Naturalistic Case	In vivo naturalistic case for an existing theory	In vivo naturalistic case for a new theory
Post Facto Naturalistic Case	Post facto naturalistic case for an existing theory	Post facto naturalistic case for a new theory

Source: Reigeluth, C. M., & Frick, T. W. (1999).

1. Select a design theory. [Not applicable if the aim is to develop theory.]
2. Design an instance of the theory or create a case to help generate a design theory.
3. Collect and analyze formative data on the instance.
4. Revise the instance
5. Repeat the data collection and revision cycle.
6. Offer tentative revisions of theory [or fully develop tentative theory].

Although this scheme may be useful, to our knowledge it has not been adopted by researchers beyond the work of the researchers who originated it and their students.

Gravemeijer & Cobb (2006). This reference provides a well-developed and specific framework for conceptualizing, planning, conducting, and reporting design research (see also Cobb et al., 2003a). It is particularly strong in describing the process of data collection and analysis and providing a rationale for that process, which is a limitation of other frameworks. Further, the authors draw on their use of the framework in conducting research aimed at increasing students' mathematical reasoning. The framework organizes design research into three phases.

The goals of phase one are to "formulate a local instructional theory . . . clarifying the study's theoretical intent . . . [to establish] learning goals, instructional endpoints . . . and the instructional starting points" (p. 19). A local instructional theory "consists of

conjectures about a possible learning process, together with conjectures about possible means of supporting that learning process"
(p. 21). The instructional theory is local because it must also take
into account the existing culture of a classroom, the orientation of
its teacher, available materials, and so forth. To accomplish this
goal, they suggested that a researcher acts like a *bricoleur,* a French
term for a handyman who is skilled at creating useful construc-
tions from available materials. However, the larger theoretical intent must also be considered in planning during this phase. That
is, a researcher must consider how the investigation will facilitate
the discovery of broader theoretical understandings in the form of
conceptual frameworks that characterize the intervention in ways
that transcend the immediate context and that lead to what they
call "ontological representations" (see DiSessa & Cobb, 2004; item
2 in Section 1.1.2). The instructional endpoints refer to the learning goals that an intervention is designed to address, which may
require researchers to "problematize the topic under consideration
from a disciplinary perspective, and [to] ask themselves: What are
the core ideas in this domain?" (p. 19). Instructional starting points
are informed in general by the literature, if it is helpful, but also
more concretely by an assessment of where the classroom and students are in relation to the instructional goals before the intervention is introduced.

The second phase is actually conducting the design experiment aimed at testing the local theory developed in phase one
and modifying it as necessary in light of systematic data collection. Data collection in this phase is cyclical as represented in Figure 2.1. The microlevel daily cycles consist of instructional moves,
which the authors characterize as hypothesis testing, followed by
reflections and debriefings with teachers and among members
of a research team, which informs the next cycle of implementing the intervention. The macrolevel cycles represent longer-term
findings, perhaps across a study, a series of studies, or parallel
classrooms in the same study. The goal of this phase is to form
emergent interpretative frameworks for understanding the intervention the local context but also ultimately in more general theoretical terms.

The authors call the third phase *retrospective analysis.* The goal
is to conduct a meta-analysis of all the data toward consolidating theoretical understandings and presumably toward draw-

ing conclusions and making recommendations. In the authors' own use of this framework, they employed "a variant of Glaser and Strauss's (1967) constant comparative method" (p. 38) to accept and refute conjectures in their analysis, looking for pivotal episodes, which are typically included in their research reports. Whatever approach is used to analyze the data in this phase, the essential goal is to document the research team's learning process and the conclusions that can be drawn from that process. Another goal or perspective in this phase is to reconstruct the local learning theory proposed at the outset in phase one.

We believe that although there are some gaps in this framework and that it lacks specificity in some area, it is a significant step toward defining more precisely the actual methods for conducting what in this book we have labeled formative and design experiments, but what others, including Gravemeijer and Cobb (2006) refer to as design research.

Bannan-Ritland (2003). Bannan-Ritland's framework is broader in scope, because it goes beyond conducting a single investigation. She referred to this overarching framework as integrative learning design (ILD). Relevant to the audience for this book, she has used the ILD framework to investigate the implementation of online support for teachers, tutors, and parents in order to foster collaborative reading with children who have disabilities (Bannan-Ritland, 2002). She summarized the overall purpose of her framework as follows:

> [The ILD] framework attempts to move past isolated, individual efforts of design research by articulating a logically ordered, but dynamic frame that considers both field studies and experimental research methodologies in advancing the systemic impact of research across a variety of domains and social settings. . . . [It] draws from traditions of instructional design . . . product design . . . usage centered design . . . and diffusion of innovations . . . as well as established educational research methodologies. ILD strives to combine the creativity of design communities with appropriate adherence to standards of quantitative and qualitative methods in education. (p. 21)

The framework consists of four distinct phases, each comprised of several specific research activities, summarized in Figure

2.4. The first phase is *informed exploration*, which is subdivided into identifying and defining the problem and surveying the literature. This phase points to one of the unique emphases of this framework: The investigation is grounded in a problem or pedagogical challenge that is established and defined from the outset, as opposed to other approaches intent on investigating, for example, how a promising intervention might be implemented successfully in particular contexts, although the promising intervention might also be justified on the basis that it confronts a pedagogical problem or challenge. Theory plays a role during this phase, although unlike Gravemeijer and Cobb's (2006) framework described in the previous section, it is not central. Instead, this framework employs a needs analysis, which is more closely associated with instructional design. However, integrating the needs of the ultimate users of an intervention into a framework for conducting a formative or design experiment increases the chances that the intervention resulting from the investigation will actually be used, which, we believe, is a strength of this framework.

In the *enactment phase* an intervention is implemented. The intervention is viewed as "a socially constructed object that must be systematically articulated and revised over a number of cycles" (p. 23). Further, Bannan-Ritland characterized development in this phase as "primarily influenced by evaluations conducted on the local impact of the intervention . . . that may last for a considerable period of time and involve multiple design cycles" (p. 23). Thus, this phase is quite similar to the second phase in Gravemeijer and Cobb's (2006) framework.

The third and fourth phases of the framework involve evaluation. In the *local impact phase*, a researcher asks "How well does

Figure 2.4. Bannan-Ritland's Integrative Learning Design (ILD)

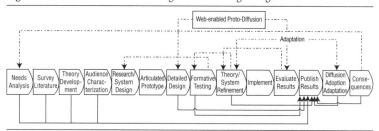

Source: Bannan-Ritland, B. (2003).

the designed intervention satisfy its clients, . . . [that is] teachers, parents, literacy facilitators, and children?" (p. 23). Data collection and analysis at this stage "are an iterative process in which formative evaluation of the intervention interacts with local theory development during an extended implementation phase including . . . more summative evaluation of the study's results and products" (p. 23). We find her description of this phase useful, but it also raises a question not clearly addressed in any of the existing frameworks: When does a researcher complete the iterative cycles of data collection and analysis and the fine-tuning of the intervention?

The fourth phase, *broader impact,* is unique to this framework, adding, we believe, not only a useful phase for conducting formative and design experiments but also an important emphasis to the ultimate goal of education researchers in general. As Bannan-Ritland stated:

> The ILD framework extends the typical "dissemination" phase of educational research in which publication or presentation of findings is sometimes seen as a closure event. . . . [Instead] ILD directs attention . . . at concerns related to the adoption (and adaptation) of researched practices and interventions [by considering] . . . the consequences and use of the products of the research. (p. 23)

Thus, built into the framework is an effort not only to disseminate the results of an investigation but also to determine whether it produces what have been termed lethal or productive mutations when it acquires wider use independent of researchers' control. A researcher's final task is to monitor how the results of his or her data-based conclusions are applied in a broader context without direct involvement of a researcher or research team. We find this final phase importantly consistent with what U.S. government funding initiatives currently refer to as scaling up interventions from small-scale, more localized trials in scientific experimentation to a broader use. However, it does so from what we believe to be a more realistically flexible perspective and is grounded in contingent rather than absolute recommendations.

Sloane and Gorard (2003). This framework is less explicit than the others offered in this section. Nonetheless, we include it because it is based on a perspective that might be useful in guiding methodological choices when conducting a formative or design experiment. The foundation of this framework is that building models is the essence of all research. Thus, conceptualizing design experiments as a model-building activity may enhance the validity of this approach, especially among researchers more invested in scientific experimentation (see Shavelson et al., 2003). The key methodological idea that this framework contributes is that model building means embracing the concept of failure. That is, engineers explicitly consider the conditions under which a designed model will fail. As they stated, "[Designers' or engineers'] goals reside in understanding failure, building better practical theory . . . and building things that work. . . . No matter the method used to test a design, the central underlying principle of this work is to obviate failure" (p. 31). Obviating failure, to us, seems like a legitimate and potentially rich idea, because it diverges radically from the perspective that guides most education research. It is also a concept that Pressley and colleagues (2006) suggested as one way to improve intervention research from their perspective as literacy researchers. It also counterbalances the narrow views and false expectations associated with the idea that there are best practices guaranteed to work if implemented with fidelity in almost any context (see Reinking, 2007).

In their brief article, Sloane and Gorard offered only a rough outline of how the concept of model building might be incorporated into design experiments, and they did not provide specific examples. In the broadest terms, the process involves model formulation followed by model estimation and validation. Model formulation in their view is grounded in fundamental statistical concepts consisting of the following (p. 30):

1. Consult, collaborate, and discuss with appropriate experts on the given topic, ask lots of questions, and most importantly listen.
2. Incorporate background theory, not only to suggest which variables to include and in what form, but also to indicate constraints on the variables and known limiting behavior.
3. Collect and then examine the data to assess their more important features.
4. Incorporate information from other similar data sets.

5. Check that a model formulated on empirical or theoretical (or both) grounds is consistent with any qualitative knowledge of the system.

6. Remember that all models are approximate and tentative . . . and be prepared to modify a model during the analysis or as further data are collected and examined.

Further, they noted that "at all stages of model formulation it is helpful to distinguish further between (a) what is known with near certainty, (b) what is reasonable to assume, and (c) what is unknown" (p. 30).

In model estimation and validation, they emphasize the limits of all models and the fact that all models, including statistical ones, need to be tempered with a commitment to what is sensible, which is, to us, a refreshing perspective given, in some quarters, the unmitigated confidence in statistical analyses to be the final arbiter of good instruction. Validation in their view involves determining the utility of a model in terms of how well it produces design principles that can be applied to other data sets. Their fundamental argument is that model building is a neglected topic among education researchers, who tend to focus on the estimation, fit, and validation of models using statistical tools, as opposed to the more fundamental process of formulating conceptual models in the first place. They see design experiments as a natural way to restore balance between these disjoint model-building endeavors.

Reinking and Bradley (2004; see also Baumann, Dillon, Schockley, Alvermann, & Reinking, 1996). We are obviously most familiar with and partial to our own framework, which we present here. It is derived from the literature pertaining specifically to formative experiments, particularly Jacob (1992) and Newman (1990, 1992), although we believe our framework also fits conceptually and methodologically into the literature explicating design experiments. It originated in our efforts to translate broad conceptual understandings of formative experiments into a more specific organizational scheme that would enable us to systematically and explicitly conceptualize, conduct, and report our research using this approach. The framework has also been adopted by other literacy researchers who have conducted and published formative experiments (Ivey & Broaddus, 2007; Lenski, 2001).

The framework is comprised of the following six questions, which are each followed by a brief explanation with examples, mainly from our own work:

   1. *What is the pedagogical goal to be investigated, why is that goal valued and important, and what theory and previous empirical work speak to accomplishing that goal instructionally?* We believe that this question is foundational to conducting formative and design experiments. Researchers should be able to articulate clearly the pedagogical goal they are seeking to address, a rationale for its importance, and the theory and previous research that underlies efforts to accomplish it.

   For example, in one of our studies (Reinking & Watkins, 2000), a goal was to increase the amount and diversity of independent reading supported in part by Stanovich's (1986) hypothesized Matthew effects, which argues that differences in reading ability are exacerbated as students advance through the elementary grades because good readers read progressively more and poor readers progressively less (i.e., the rich get richer and the poor get poorer). Likewise, there is a considerable literature pointing out that the required book report is a ubiquitous, but largely ineffective, even counterproductive, instructional response in many classrooms. In another study (Bradley, 2004) the goal was to increase the amount and quality of verbal interactions between children and teachers in a preschool setting. Previous findings indicated that a relatively low percentage of such interactions were semantically rich (Dickinson & Tabors, 2001), and there have been theoretical arguments suggesting that such interactions are related to later literacy development (Snow, Burns, & Griffin, 1998; Storch & Whitehurst, 2002).

   2. *What intervention, consistent with a guiding theory, has the potential to achieve the pedagogical goal and why?* An intervention—which may include procedures, approaches, materials, and so forth—is at the heart of a formative or design experiment. The intervention might be an established one that has been the object of research employing other methodologies (e.g., semantic mapping as an approach to integrating new vocabulary into students' conceptual schema), an adaptation of an established intervention (e.g., applying reciprocal teaching to developing reading comprehension on

the Internet), or a collection of alternative, but related, interventions that might be employed to address a single pedagogical goal (e.g., various strategies embedded within daily school activities aimed at increasing the amount and quality of verbal interaction in preschool classrooms). Alternatively, the intervention might be entirely new, developed specifically to address the pedagogical goal and in conformance to the rationale and theory justifying that goal. For example, in the Reinking and Watkins (2000) study the intervention involved creating multimedia book reviews as an alternative to the conventional book report (see also Lehrer & Schauble, 2004, for an example of a newly constructed intervention aimed at increasing statistical reasoning and students' intuitive awareness of statistical concepts).

3. *What factors enhance or inhibit the effectiveness, efficiency, and appeal of the intervention in regard to achieving the set pedagogical goal?* Whereas the previous two questions in our framework are foundational to conceptualizing a formative experiment, this question and subsequent questions are foundational to data collection, analysis, and interpretation. That is, the methodological essence of formative and design experiments is the collection of data aimed at determining what works, what doesn't, and why. More importantly, addressing those questions is key to testing, developing, and refining theoretical understandings and thus making specific recommendations about instructional practice. To address this question in the framework, a researcher must employ appropriate and convincing methods and approaches to characterize the environment within which the investigation takes place (typically through ethnographic methods) and to identify what factors are critical in producing desirable outcomes. We believe that methodological and analytical flexibility is reasonable in addressing this question, but others are likely to seek more specificity in order to establish rigor (e.g., Gravemeijer & Cobb's [2006] framework, presented previously).

For example, in the Reinking and Watkins (2000) study observational data, including the identification of purposefully selected focal students, interviews with the teachers, and focus group interviews, revealed that poor readers in one fourth-grade class resisted getting involved in what other students saw as appealing and engaging computer-based activities. Our data also revealed an explanation: Because the activity involved creating reviews of books for a database available for use in the school media center, the poor readers did not wish to display their lack of reading ability by entering only books well below grade level. In the Bradley (2004) study, lunchroom conversations that provided a rich opportunity for verbal interactions were stifled because of restrictions on noise levels and teachers' strong beliefs that the children needed to eat well at lunch because of poor nutrition at home. Accommodating those factors is the object of the next question in the framework.

4. How can the intervention be modified to achieve the pedagogical goal more effectively and efficiently and in a way that is appealing and engaging to all stakeholders? This question works in tandem with the previous question to form an iterative cycle of data-driven instructional moves (the microcycles in the Gravemeijer & Cobb [2006] framework; see Figure 2.1). In other words, when factors that enhance and inhibit an intervention's effectiveness, efficiency, and appeal are identified and explained, the intervention is modified accordingly to capitalize on the enhancing factors and to circumvent or neutralize the inhibiting factors. Data are then gathered to determine whether an instructional move accomplished its intended purpose. Extending the example introduced under the previous question, the teacher of the poor readers who resisted advertising their weaker reading skills by entering multimedia book reviews of below-grade-level books into a public database came up with a viable solution. She suggested to students that there was a need for easier books in the database for younger children in the lower grades. That seemed to sanction their involvement and indeed overcame their resistance, which was documented in our data to further establish the validity of the original interpretation of the reasons for their lack of involvement. Reading ability thus emerged as a critical factor in the success of the intervention.

5. What unanticipated positive and negative effects does the intervention produce? Some of the observed effects of an intervention are noteworthy and important even if they do not directly influence the accomplishment of a pedagogical goal (see item 5 in Section 2.3). Teachers know that instruction produces unintended consequences that can sometimes be as important or more important than the primary intent of instruction. Our framework specifically acknowledges that reality and incorporates it systematically into data collection, analysis, and interpretation. For example, in the Reinking and Watkins (2000) study, we found that low-achieving special education students exhibited a different persona during the activities related to the intervention when compared to other times during the schoolday.

6. Has the instructional environment changed as a result of the intervention? This question is included in our framework because of the ecological orientation of formative and design experiments. In addition, the interventions studied are often selected with an eye toward positively transforming educational perspectives or the cultural milieu of the classroom beyond simply accomplishing a narrow pedagogical goal (see Newman, 1990, 1992). For example, in the Reinking and Watkins (2000) study the intervention had implications for the way teachers viewed students' independent reading, their responses to literature, and the integration of technology into instruction. One consequential finding of practical and theoretical importance was that the intervention was less successful in schools where the administrative climate was top-down and heavy-handed, which seemed to stifle creativity and to limit effects of the intervention and to confine those effects to a rather narrow space in the curriculum and schoolday.

In addition to addressing these six questions, we have planned and conducted our formative experiments in several phases:

- Phase 1 is a preliminary phase during which we recruit schools and teachers, meet with appropriate stakeholders, and discuss with them the goals of the project as well as the obligations and responsibilities of those involved; when teachers have agreed to participate, we negotiate plans for implementing the subsequent phases of the project, including the intervention.
- Phase 2 involves gathering demographic data; we use ethnographic methods to create a thick description of the classroom, school, and community; and we interview teachers and other stakeholders.

- Phase 3 consists of gathering baseline data to establish where participants are in relation to our pedagogical goal prior to implementing an intervention.
- Phase 4, the heart of the investigation, involves implementing the intervention and gathering data that speak to questions 3–6 in our framework.
- Phase 5 is a postassessment to provide a point of comparison with the baseline data gathered in phase 3.
- Phase 6 involves consolidating findings (similar to the retrospective analysis in the Gravemeijer & Cobb [2006] framework) and writing up results.

2.5. WHAT PRACTICAL, ETHICAL, AND METHODOLOGICAL ISSUES HAVE WE ENCOUNTERED IN USING THIS APPROACH?

Any approach to research entails ethical, methodological, and practical issues that challenge researchers using that approach. Many of these issues revolve around the nitty-gritty details or unique situations with which researchers must contend but which are not often addressed in books and articles about research methodology. Without such guidance, individual researchers must often sort through these issues ad hoc from study to study, often while they are in the midst of a research project. This inattention to more practical issues is also the case, we believe, with formative and design experiments, perhaps more so because that approach has not yet acquired full methodological clarity. In this section we highlight a few such issues we have encountered in our work using this approach, acknowledging that a more comprehensive examination is needed, but that is beyond the scope of this book.

2.5.1. What stance should a researcher take in classrooms and working with teachers?

A researcher's presence and role in classrooms and how he or she relates to teachers raises important issues, or ought to, we believe, regardless of the methodology used to study classroom phenomena. However, those issues are particularly important for researchers who employ formative or design experiments, because it is an approach that requires researchers to enter deeply into the ecology of a classroom, often with the aim of transforming teaching and learning. To some degree a researcher becomes a purposeful agent of change. To serve that role, a researcher must inevitably work closely with teachers to implement instructional activities aimed at accomplishing a specific goal and bringing about positive change, which complicates the ethical, methodological, and logistical issues associated with this approach.

We believe that in general the most realistic and justifiable role for a researcher conducting a formative and design experiment is that of a participant-observer (Creswell, 2002) in a classroom. That is, in our experience it is unrealistic for a researcher to be simply a dispassionate observer or consultant largely disengaged from the activities and interactions taking place in a classroom, although there may be times and situations that warrant taking on more strictly the role of an observer.

For example, when engaging in participant-observation, a researcher might help to manage classroom activities, teach whole-class lessons, work with small groups of students, or work one-on-one with students. These types of interactions not only help a researcher to understand better the learning environment, the needs of the students, and the demands of teaching; they can also create opportunities for teachers to meet with students individually or in small groups or give them time to plan and prepare for lessons and other activities. We have found that teachers greatly appreciate such participation if a researcher is supporting their work and if it contributes substantively to creating a positive professional bond between researcher and teacher. Such support may extend beyond the boundaries of the project. For example, Kamberelis and de la Luna (1998) became involved in after-school functions, and in our own research we have helped with an evening technology fair (Reinking & Watkins, 2000) and have gone on field trips with the class (Bradley, 2004). We have found this involvement to enrich our understanding and to enable us to form close working relationships with teachers.

We have found it difficult to be in a classroom for an extended period of time, working closely with a teacher to implement instructional activities, and not to be a participant as well as an observer. However, that raises a key, and unresolved, methodological issue in conducting formative and design experiments: How to avoid allowing one's participation to unduly influence the ecology of the classroom or the effects of the intervention. Doing so requires walking a thin line between constructive, empathetic, collaborative support and directing activities that are essential to producing whatever effects the intervention might evoke. Put succinctly, to what extent is a researcher's presence and involvement in a classroom part of the intervention and one of the factors that may contribute to changing the ecology? Part of the answer may be broadening the framework for this approach to include an expectation that individual studies are part of a program of research that entails early studies with much research involvement and later studies with less involvement (e.g., see Bannan-Ritland's [2003] framework in Section 2.4.2).

Establishing a professional, productive, and ethical relationship with a teacher is also essential but entails even more complex and delicate issues. Thus, we believe that a researcher who conducts formative and design experiments should be well versed in the literature on collaborative research. Some good sources aimed specifically at literacy research include Kamberelis and de la Luna (1998), Snyder (1992), and Smagorinsky and Jordahl (1991). Although that literature is useful and informative, and perhaps an appropriate way to frame some investigations, we do not believe that it is necessary to consider all formative and design experiments to be collaborative research in the strictest sense. Doing so would imply that equality between the roles of a researcher and of a teacher is necessary in assuming responsibility for conducting the research. Instead, we believe that Cole and Knowles's (1993) description of what they refer to as teacher development partnership research is generally consistent with formative and design experiments. As they stated, "True collaboration is more likely to result when the aim is *not* for *equal* involvement in all aspects of the research; but, rather, for *negotiated and mutually agreed upon* involvement where strengths and available time commitments to process are honored" (p. 486, emphasis in original). They presented a matrix, reproduced in Figure 2.5, summarizing the respective roles and responsibilities of a teacher and a researcher in teacher development partnership research.

We believe that a natural and important by-product of conducting formative and design experiments is professional development. For example, in our own work we have found that teachers become more reflective about their practice and become more involved in professional development activities in the context of a formative experiment. Similarly, in their collaborative research study, Kamberelis and de la Luna (1998) found that the teacher, through their encouragement and persistence, came to appreciate her opportunity to participate in conference presentations and publications. Further, the teacher's participation in the research process became a source of professional self-esteem, even though that role was not particularly valued in her school. Thus, we believe that researchers who conduct formative and design experiments should also be well versed in the literature on teacher development (e.g., Cochran-Smith & Lytle, 1999). However, formative and design experiments are not only a stimulus for teachers' professional development. The professional development of researchers can also be enhanced by providing an opportunity to reflect on their knowledge, beliefs, and attitudes toward teachers, educational environments, and the role of education research.

Figure 2.5. Matrix for considering relationships and responsibilities in teacher development partnership research

	Planning and preparation *(purpose, procedure, access, roles, logistics of time and place)*	Information gathering *(participation, observation, interviews, taping, written accounts)*	Interpretations and representation *(verification, validation, voice)*	Reporting and use *(voice, control, benefits, public/ private use)*
Teacher (person affiliated with an institution primarily oriented toward practice)	Negotiated participation in terms of perceived benefit, commitment, and procedures	Identification of information sources and negotiation of appropriate strategies	Responsive to preliminary analyses; mutual interpretation leading to final analysis	Negotiated representation in report and editing of personal accounts; perceived mutual benefit
Researcher (person affiliated with a research institution)	Primary responsibility for articulation of purpose, coordination of research, and negotiation of activities	Identification of possible strategies and primary responsibility for gathering mutually agreed-upon information	Preparation and presentation of preliminary analysis; mutual interpretation of preliminary analysis leading to final analysis	Primary responsibility for writing account; responsive to teachers' editorial and representational comments; perceived mutual benefits

Source: Cole, A. L., & Knowles, J. G. (1993).

Cole and Knowles (1993) also identified useful categories for researchers to consider when planning and conducting teacher development partnership research: (1) technical issues, including financial support and logistics of timing and place; (2) personnel issues, including the specific responsibilities of the teacher and how those responsibilities will be managed; (3) ethical issues, including issues of confidentiality; (4) political issues, including how participation in the study may affect a teacher's professional life and standing in a school; and (5) educational issues, including how participation may contribute to a teacher's professional development. We believe these are useful categories for researchers to consider in laying the groundwork for conducting a formative or design experiment. Further, the categories illustrate that the issues involved in conducting a formative and design experiment in classrooms are decidedly complex and need to be approached by researchers who are well grounded in the relevant literature, who are sensitive to the complex interacting factors that must be attended to in creating a healthy but not distracting presence in a classroom, and who are respectful of the ecology of a classroom and of the professional knowledge and prerogatives of teachers.

2.5.2. How do researchers find and set up an appropriate site for research?

This question is an extension of the previous one and is the essential question underlying the first phase in our framework presented in Section 2.4.2. Once a researcher has created an alignment among a pedagogical goal, a rationale for its importance, relevant theoretical and empirical background, and an intervention to investigate, the next logical step is to find a site for the research. As we discussed in Section 2.3 (item 6), we believe that the selection of an appropriate research site is a dimension of establishing rigor, and we discuss in that section some of the characteristics of an ideal site.

However, as with most methodological decisions, trade-offs are often necessary between finding an ideal site and finding one that is available and willing to participate. For example, in our recent work, it has been difficult to find sites willing to make room for an intervention unless administrators can be convinced that the intervention is likely to contribute directly to increasing scores on high-stakes tests, particularly in schools with high percentages of students with relatively low achievement in reading. Interestingly, even when schools agree to participate, that stance typically becomes a prominent factor in determining how the intervention is implemented, modified, and ultimately furthers our pedagogical goals.

Once a district, school, or classroom becomes a candidate for becoming a research site, a researcher must be savvy about negotiating possible involvement in a study. All researchers who conduct research in schools must understand the ways schools operate and how teachers and administrators think and what constraints they must accommodate. Obviously, it is useful if a researcher conducting a formative or design experiment has served in one of those roles or will include someone who does on a research team. It is also helpful if a researcher has a friendly and cooperative demeanor and can communicate a genuine interest in forming an ongoing professional relationship with a teacher, school, and district. We believe that researchers who wish to conduct formative and design experiments need an extra measure of these sensitivities and qualities to be successful in finding appropriate research sites and negotiating teachers' and schools' involvement in their research. However, again, we are not aware of any resources that explicitly discuss these aspects of research or any systematic inclusion of this topic in preparing doctoral students to be researchers.

Ideally, once a district, school, and teacher have participated and have had an agreeable experience, they will be inclined to participate in further studies. Thus, carefully and systematically cultivating and negotiating involvement in a formative or design experiment initially will lay the groundwork for conducting a program of research over many years.

Our practice has been to initiate contact with a school principal at schools that meet various criteria derived from our pedagogical goals, the nature of the intervention, and so forth. For example, we may target schools with a high percentage of students who qualify for a free or reduced-price lunch, schools that have needed resources, or perhaps those that do not, if our intent is to consider how an intervention might or might not work in less-than-ideal circumstances. We meet with the principal to outline the parameters of the project. If the principal is open, and hopefully enthusiastic, we suggest a meeting with teachers who might be interested in participating. If the principal mentions the need for district office approval, we seek that approval. We are careful to ensure that administrators will not strong-arm teachers to participate. When there has been administrative approval, we then meet with teachers to overview the project, including outlining our pedagogical goals, the planned intervention, a broad conceptual introduction to formative and design experiments, and what the obligations and potential benefits of participation will be. We also emphasize that we are interested in determining how the intervention can be accommodated into their teaching and curriculum and that we do not intend to inflexibly impose the intervention on them and their students.

Perhaps the most basic requirement for enlisting a particular teacher in a formative or design experiment is ensuring that there is some genuine investment in the goals, intentions, and potential outcomes as well as a willingness to have some flexibility in accommodating the intervention in instruction. That requirement means that a researcher must be prepared to articulate clearly the pedagogical goal and to determine whether there is support, if not enthusiasm, for achieving it, and whether there is reasonable flexibility in accommodating the intervention in existing instruction. A researcher must also be explicit about the obligations and responsibilities for a participating school, classroom, or teacher as well as about potential benefits. These issues are likely to be the subject of a follow-up conversation with an interested teacher before a final agreement on participation is reached.

Once a researcher has enlisted a teacher or set of teachers in the project, it is necessary specifically to discuss the intervention and the logistical details of implementing it and of collecting data. At this point, a researcher needs to be particularly sensitive to a teacher's values, orientations, and circumstances, putting aside preconceived notions about exactly how the intervention *ought* to be carried out. Although there may be a core of nonnegotiable elements and pedagogical principles without which the intervention would no longer exist, in our view a researcher should have as much flexibility as possible in accommodating a teacher's wishes and circumstances, both in how the intervention is initially implemented and how the data are collected. In fact, in one sense, these initial accommodations are a preliminary test of the intervention's viability and the way it may need to be adapted to accommodate teachers' needs, values, and preferences. Some tensions at points during the project may be inevitable and need to be dealt with delicately and sensitively. Snyder (1992) and Yaden and Tam (2000) discussed the difficulties faced by researchers when their agendas may compete with the agendas of the teachers with whom they work and how that tension might be accommodated.

As this process and the issues it creates illustrate, researchers conducting a formative and design experiment clearly need to continuously cultivate and maintain a positive, supportive, and professionally respectful and enriching professional relationship with the teachers with whom they work. Researchers conducting formative and design experiments need to realize that it takes time to develop a shared understanding of key ideas and concepts, to define relevant instructional issues or problems, to allow instructional practices to evolve and dissolve in light of contextual factors, and to develop a trust that fully acknowledges each other's limitations (see Wilson & Berne, 1999).

2.5.3. Can a researcher also be the teacher in a formative or design experiment?

This question applies to two different circumstances. First is the circumstance in which the researcher is indeed the teacher, that is, where the researcher is not simply assuming the role of a teacher in another teacher's class. We are ambivalent about whether that circumstance is appropriate methodologically. Such situations may be more appropriately considered to be in the realm of action research (see Burnaford, Fischer, & Hobson, 2001), but an investigation under that circumstance may nonetheless follow an orientation and a framework consistent with formative and design experiments, which is different from action research (see Section 1.1.3). We are familiar with two such studies in literacy research, one by Duffy (2001) and one by Garfield (2000), which may be instructive for those who wish to explore this issue.

The other circumstance is one in which a researcher assumes the main responsibility for implementing an intervention with a classroom teacher's students (e.g., Jiménez, 1997). Doing so raises methodological issues of validity, as discussed in previous sections. Specifically, to what extent does the researcher become part of the intervention and to what extent are findings dependent on a researcher, who is often highly committed to and well versed in the intervention? On the other hand, is it a fair test of the intervention's potential use and effectiveness if it is implemented inappropriately or in an unskilled fashion? One way we have addressed this dilemma is through compromise. We have asked teachers whether they want to implement the intervention or whether they would like us to implement it and proceed accordingly. Or we have worked in several classrooms with varying levels of researcher involvement in teaching, which provides a useful contrast. Or we have taken the lead in an initial investigation, and then turned things over to a teacher in a subsequent replication in a separate study. Teachers may also be easier to recruit if a researcher offers to take the lead for developing and implementing the content of the intervention, particularly if the intervention entails complicated logistical issues (e.g., using computers) or the development of original materials and activities. However, if a teacher wishes to take the lead from the outset, a researcher may need to provide in-service preparation, which raises issues of teachers' time and how to compensate them for that extra time.

2.5.4. When should the intervention phase end?

Another methodological issue often influenced by practical circumstances is deciding when to end an investigation, particularly in relation to a pedagogical goal and the effectiveness of the intervention. As discussed in Section 2.3, a criterion for establishing the rigor of a formative or design experiment is adequate time to implement the intervention. Even given progress toward achieving a goal, at what point might the goal be considered achieved or progress demonstrable and considered adequate? That question may be addressed in part by including a control or alternate treatment group in the design as a point of comparison. Further, at what point might a researcher determine that there are unlikely to be further notable improvements in the way the intervention is implemented? Is there something equivalent to the concept of saturation in qualitative data analysis, where new data are producing no new themes or findings, or, in the case of a formative and design experiment, where there are only incremental improvements in the intervention? Obviously, some practical concerns may dictate when an investigation ends making such questions moot. For example, the school year ends or funding expires.

2.5.5. How do the results of a formative or design experiment complement other approaches to research?

Working within the context of a larger project employing other research methodologies also raises the issue of how the results of a formative and design experiment might merge logically with other methodologies. For example, in a 3-year federally funded project (Leu & Reinking, 2005) studying how reciprocal teaching might be adapted to develop reading comprehension on the Internet, year 2 was proposed as a formative experiment aimed at refining the intervention and identifying factors that might be studied or controlled in a more conventional scientific experiment to be conducted in year 3. Such an approach is consistent with some views of the role that formative and design experiments play in the field's literature base (e.g., see McCandliss et al., 2003). That is, formative and design experiments provide preliminary data that can guide conventional controlled experimentation or field trials. On the other hand, a different logic might suggest a reversal of that order. That is, if an intervention shows promise under the highly constrained and purposefully controlled conditions of a conventional experiment under laboratory-like conditions, a formative or design experiment might provide information about the conditions of its effectiveness under a variety of more authentic environments where variables are not closely controlled. That logic is more consistent with Brown's (1992) original conception of design experiments as an extension of her controlled laboratory experiments, but we also believe it is reasonable to start with design experiments, moving to subsequent studies that are more controlled.

2.5.6. How do researchers deal with troubling information?

Formative and design experiments, because they typically entail deep involvement in the culture of a classroom and school as well as in the lives of teachers and students, often present a researcher with ethical dilemmas and decisions. For example, in one study our work inadvertently revealed that a young child was being sexually abused at home. In another study, a principal threatened a teacher with a transfer if she did not consent to participate in the study for a second year, because the principal saw our project as an important component of an application to become a school of excellence in a state competition. We have occasionally observed teachers engage in unprofessional behavior. In one report of our work, several factors that we identified as inhibiting the success of the intervention had the potential to reflect negatively on a teacher, although we took care to present these data without being judgmental. Prior to submitting our work for publication, we always submit a draft to the teachers with whom we have worked and to the school principal, inviting their comments and giving them the option to write a disclaimer or minority report. Although none have decided to do so, should we receive such a response, we would include it as part of a manuscript submitted for publication.

There are also ethical dimensions to deciding when it is appropriate to consider teachers as part of the research team and consequently when to include them as authors on publications. That may be particularly problematic when working in several classrooms where some teachers are engaged more substantively in the research than others but where inviting some, but not others, to be co-authors may create professional and interpersonal tensions. The need to navigate these and similar ethical issues is not uncommon when conducting formative and design experiments, and dealing with such issues requires a researcher using this approach to carefully navigate intrapersonal, professional, and ethical considerations.

CHAPTER 3

What Are Some Good Examples of Formative and Design Experiments?

3.1. WHY IS IT DIFFICULT TO FIND AND SELECT GOOD EXAMPLES?

Although formative and design experiments surfaced in the early 1990s, there have been relatively few published, peer-reviewed studies clearly identified with that approach. Thus, there is a relatively small pool of possible examples, and published studies are not always easy to locate for several reasons. First, there is the issue of terminology. Using key words to search for studies is problematic because of the many different terms used to describe this approach to research. As discussed in Section 1.1.1, we have used the term *formative and design experiments*, but other researchers, particularly more recently, have used other terms. Second, this approach has been employed across several fields of study in education and published in diverse outlets. There is no journal devoted specifically to publishing formative or design experiments, although *The Journal of the Learning Sciences* (http://www.cc.gatech.edu/lst/jls), sponsored by the International Society of the Learning Sciences (http://www.isls.org), is an outlet that has a strand on "Design Study/Design Experiment Methodology," and the sponsoring organization is a "professional society dedicated to the interdisciplinary empirical investigation of learning as it exists in real-world settings." Finally, as one of the reviewers of an earlier draft of our book pointed out, this approach has been adopted internationally and published examples are not always readily available in the most widely used searchable databases such as the Educational Resources Information Center

(ERIC) in the United States. Nonetheless, we have tried to create a comprehensive, if not exhaustive, list of studies using this approach published in research journals. We list the published, peer-reviewed literacy studies we have found in Figure 3.2 and studies in other areas in Figure 3.3.

In addition, it is not clear within this set of studies which of them might be cited as prototypical examples exhibiting notable conceptual soundness and methodological rigor (see Section 2.2). We do not believe that currently there would be a clear consensus among researchers using this approach about which studies are good examples to be emulated and which may be marginal examples suggesting a more rudimentary or incomplete conceptual and methodological understanding. The status of design and formative experiments as an emerging approach to research that originated from diverse sources and that has embraced methodological flexibility may explain that lack of clarity. Likewise, there may currently be too few examples in the literature for a clear consensus about exemplars to emerge.

We attempt to deal with that ambiguity in Figure 3.1, which we offer as a preliminary step toward clarifying what studies might be offered as good examples. The intent of the taxonomy in Figure 3.1 is not to make definitive judgments about the appropriateness or quality of existing studies, nor to sort all existing studies into the respective cells, although we could imagine doing so if an operational definition was created for each cell. Instead, the taxonomy is offered here as a conceptual touchstone. That is, we introduce it only as an avenue to opening discussions that might eventually lead to more precise, consensual understandings about the essence of this new approach and how it might be exercised appropriately and rigorously.

The columns separate research that claims or does not claim to be a formative or design experiment (or with some similar term such as *design study*). Indeed, we have found a few studies that we would classify as consistent with formative or design experiments that are not described as formative or design experiments (or with any related terms), which perhaps continues to validate their intuitive appeal among diverse researchers. The rows separate studies that include many or few of the defining characteristics of formative and design experiments as outlined in Section 1.1.2. In three of the cells, we cite studies that will be highlighted subsequently in this chapter as examples of their respective categories without implying that they are necessarily the best overall examples, conceptually or methodologically.

Logically, the cell in the lower-right quadrant includes all studies using other methodologies, and it is therefore not particularly relevant to the present discussion. However, it does acknowledge that studies using more conventional approaches and methodologies might conceivably incorporate some of the characteristics of formative and design experiments. For example, a conventional quantitative or qualitative study might collect data to determine whether a teaching environment is transformed in some way by an instructional intervention or it might take a decidedly flexible methodological stance.

We wish to emphasize that our intent is not to be critical of studies that fall into the lower-left quadrant or imply that they are of inferior quality or necessarily bad examples. The studies in that quadrant may be important, valid, and rigorous in their own right. The question simply becomes: Are they clear examples of formative or design experiments, as they have come to be understood at this point in time? Studies in that quadrant may simply reflect that the methods of formative and design experiments are evolving and need further clarification. Nonetheless, we would expect that as the methods of formative and design experiments become better articulated and understood, there will be more consensus about their defining characteristics and thus more exemplary studies will fall into the upper-left quadrant. For the time being, it is not clear whether formative and design experiments must have all or only a few, perhaps essential, defining characteristics (see Section 1.1.2) to be considered good examples of this methodology.

3.2. What Studies Illustrate the Diversity of this Approach?

In this section we provide examples of literacy studies that fall into each of the three most relevant cells of Figure 3.1. Further, Figure 3.2 summarizes the published, peer-reviewed studies we could locate that (1) focus on interventions pertaining to literacy, and (2) are described as either a formative or design experiment. Each study in Figure 3.2 is characterized in relation to the six defining characteristics of formative and design experiments elaborated upon in Section 1.1.2. Finally, we briefly discuss peer-reviewed studies published in outlets for practitioners.

Figure 3.1. A conceptual taxonomy of formative and design experiments with
representative studies

	Studies that claim to be formative or design experiments	Studies that do not claim to be formative or design experiments
Studies with many of the defining characteristics of formative and design experiments	Lenski (2001) Palinscar, Magnusson, Collins, & Cutter (2001)	Hacker & Tenent (2002) Yaden & Tam (2000)
Studies with few or none of the defining characteristics of formative and design experiments	De Corte, Verschaffel, & van de Ven (2001) Welch (2000)	Studies using other methodologies that may have some characteristics of formative and design experiments.

Studies with many defining characteristics. Lenski's (2001) formative experiment investigated a third-grade teacher's questioning
strategies as she purposefully attempted to increase the number
and type of intertextual connections students made during post-
reading discussions. Thus, her investigation had a clear pedagogical goal. By merging ideas from a transactional theory of reading,
constructivism, and semiotics, she framed her study by the following premises: (1) the intertextual links that readers make are
situated in individual learners, (2) a discussion is itself a textual
site that is used as a resource for constructing meaning, and (3) using a variety of intertextual questions creates more possibilities for
meaning making. Thus, her study represented an conscious alignment of theory, intervention, and practice that Hoadley (2004)
argued is the basis for methodological rigor in design research,
although her study was not explicitly aimed at testing theory.

To facilitate students' comprehension, the teacher in her study
was asked to implement an intervention referred to as directed
reading–connecting activity (DR–CA), a questioning strategy that
involves several key prompts. Her study was conducted across 6
months, thus meeting one of the criteria for rigor outlined in Section
2.3. Specifically, the teacher asked students questions to facilitate
their understanding of a text by making intratextual, intertextual,
and extratextual connections. Further, before implementing the intervention, Lenski (2001) and the teacher met to discuss (1) how

the study would be conducted, (2) how the intervention strategy would be implemented, and (3) each participant's role in the study. Thus, her work aligns with Cole and Knowles's (1993) teacher development partnership research, discussed in Section 2.5.1, and our belief that extensive groundwork needs to be laid before data are collected (Section 2.5.2).

During the study, the teacher adapted the intervention by writing questions related to the DR-CA framework in advance, which she believed allowed her to respond better to the needs of her students during the discussion. The teacher also began to reflect on the types of questions facilitated and responses that defined good intertextual connections. Through that process, the teacher came to the conclusion that it was important "to have a clear understanding of the story and how it related to the curriculum before she began the discussion" (Lenski, 2001, p. 329). This understanding led the teacher to further adapt the intervention by creating graphic organizers with four types of intertextual questions plus a space to add questions that related specifically to the curriculum. Thus, there was clearly an adaptive and iterative approach to implementing the intervention.

Lenski (2001) described two unanticipated effects resulting from the implementation of the intervention, and they illustrate an interest in determining how the intervention transformed the environment. First, the teacher reconceptualized her purposes for having discussions about literature. That is, the teacher realized that she did not always need to lead the discussion but instead could follow the lead of her students. A second unanticipated effect was that the teacher developed a new respect for and confidence in her own ability to ask questions, as opposed to relying on teacher's manuals. Further, the teacher came to realize that she often dominated the discussions and "she made efforts to allow students more opportunities to talk, to question each other, and to initiate topics for discussion" (Lenski, 2001, p. 330). The teacher also began to allow and encourage students to share the role of discussion leader, which, at times, led to questions beyond the teacher's knowledge as well as created opportunities for richer intertextual connections.

Finally, qualitative methods were used to conduct this study. Although methodological flexibility was not evident, qualitative data, critical to formative and design experiments, was systematically collected, analyzed, and used to identify (1) factors that facilitated or inhibited the intervention, (2) unanticipated effects, and (3) changes in the classroom environment.

A second example in this category is Palinscar, Magnusson, Collins, and Cutter's (2001) 2-year design experiment testing the hypothesis that guided inquiry supporting multiple literacies (GIsML) would be particularly beneficial for students with special needs. Specifically, their purpose was to understand the opportunities and challenges associated with guided-inquiry science instruction, and the goal of GIsML was to promote scientific understanding in upper-elementary students with special needs. Thus, this study was explicitly aimed at testing theoretical hypotheses and the intervention was goal-oriented.

During the first year, working in four classrooms, the researchers collected and analyzed videotapes, field notes, student interviews, artifacts, and teacher focus groups, as well as formal written assessments, "to serve as the grist for generating a list of teaching practices" that might be used to enhance the intervention (Palinscar et al., p. 20). During a second year, the university-based research team met with each of the four teachers to discuss the teaching practices and the findings. Focusing on (1) monitoring and facilitating students' thinking, (2) supporting students' print literacy, and (3) improving students' ability to work in groups, the researchers and teachers identified specific teaching practices that could be implemented to enhance the GIsML. Thus, the qualitative data collected in year 1 to identify factors that influenced the implementation of the intervention informed how the intervention was adapted and then implemented during year 2.

At the end of the study, the researchers analyzed students' formal written assessments and concluded in general that students during year 2 made greater gains when teachers implemented the enhanced GIsML. Further, more students made statistically significant learning gains based on pre- and posttest assessments. However, which groups of students (i.e., normally achieving students, low-achieving students, students identified with special needs) demonstrated statistically significant gains varied unexpectedly across teachers. Based on analysis of classroom observations and teacher journals, the researchers found that each teacher tended to focus on or to emphasize a particular element of the enhanced intervention. Further, the researchers recognized that the teachers' prior knowledge and ability might have affected their teaching behaviors. Thus, the methodological flexibility often associated with formative and design experiments was demonstrated in this study as qualitative and quantitative methods were used differently in years 1 and 2. The intensity and diversity of data collected over a 2-year span are also indicators of methodological rigor.

Studies with few defining characteristics. Representative of this category is De Corte, Verschaffel, and van de Ven's (2001) study, which they call a design experiment aimed at testing the hypothesis that a classroom learning environment affects students' adoption and use of reading strategies. Specifically, the purpose of their study was to develop, implement, and evaluate research-based strategies for facilitating reading comprehension of informational texts among upper-elementary students. The intervention developed, in collaboration with the teachers, included four previously researched text comprehension strategies (i.e., prior knowledge, clarifying vocabulary, schematic representation, main idea) and the use of a metacognitive strategy. Four fifth-grade teachers, during a 4-month period, taught their students how to use these strategies via modeling, whole-class discussion, and small-group work.

The data collected included classroom observations, teacher and student interviews, and standardized reading assessments. This use of mixed methods is consistent with the methodological flexibility characteristic of formative and design experiments. Similar data were collected for a control classroom. However, no attempts were made to modify the intervention. In fact, the researchers were concerned about maintaining the fidelity of the intervention, which is distinctly inconsistent with the iterative nature of formative and design experiments (see Section 1.1.2, item 4) and the cycles of data-driven moves that are at the heart of developing emerging hypotheses and theoretical understandings (see Figure 2.3). Further, although the researchers described components of the learning environment that may have helped students to make progress, there is no report of how the classroom environment may have been transformed beyond the intervention. In stating their conclusions, the authors describe their study as a quasi-experiment, and their methods may be more consistent with that approach.

A second example in this category, although it does not focus directly on literacy, is Welch's (2000) study, described in the title as using "a formative experimental approach." That study aimed to better understand team teaching and its effectiveness on fourth- and fifth-grade students' learning. Although Welch (2000) described different variations of team teaching, the theory behind those variations was not presented. Neither was there a clearly stated pedagogical goal supported by a rationale for its importance. Thus, there is no evidence that theory played a role in the study, either in justifying the intervention or as a position being tested in practice. Welch described the professional development the teachers received for implementing team teaching, but the specific components of team teaching or guidelines for implementing it were not presented. Therefore, beyond the 30 to 45 minutes of an ill-defined daily regimen of team teaching, it is unclear what the intervention entailed during this 16- to 19-week study.

The results did address a set of research questions, although these questions were posed in a way more consistent with conventional research. For example, students seemed to benefit from a team-teaching approach based on a curriculum-based reading and writing assessment, and the primary form of team-teaching engaged in by the two teams of teachers was the lead-support method. However, because the components of the team-teaching intervention were not specified, it is unclear how or why these instructional approaches came about. That is, it is not clear if these were the original components of the intervention or modifications. Although Welch (2000) presented the obstacles the teachers faced (e.g., lack of preplanning dialogue initially created inequities in power and disagreements about discipline procedures), those obstacles were presented only in relation to teachers' impressions and their satisfaction with the team-teaching approach, not in such a way as to inform how the intervention might be improved. There was no systematic analysis of the factors enhancing or inhibiting the success of the intervention. Nor was there an analysis of how those factors might figure in modifying the intervention to further the goals for its use. Likewise, there was no discussion of how team teaching might have transformed the learning environment, such as facilitating overall changes in the approach to teacher education or changing the orientations of instructors using this approach.

Studies with many defining characteristics, but not claiming to be formative or design experiments. An example in this category is Hacker and Tenent's (2002) 3-year qualitative study investigating how elementary school teachers implemented and modified reciprocal teaching (RT, which is a well-researched, theoretically grounded reading intervention to promote active, strategic reading comprehension) to better meet the needs of their students. This study was based on research findings that teachers can have difficulty implementing such interventions; therefore, the purpose of this study was to determine whether the essential elements of RT remained as teachers implemented and modified RT. Although not described as a formative or design experiment, this study examined why and how teachers modified an intervention. Specifically, for each of the 3 years, classroom observations, field notes, surveys, and feedback from teachers were used to identify obstacles that teachers encountered and modifications they made and to facilitate the development of guidelines for implementing and practicing of reciprocal teaching. During the second and third year, additional data were collected to broaden their understanding of how students and parents viewed RT. Further, students were administered standardized assessments to determine the effectiveness of RT. Consequently, this study illustrates several of the characteristics of formative and design experiments, including methodological flexibility (see Section 1.2).

During the three years of this study, Hacker and Tenent (2002) worked with a total of 24 teachers who, although encountering similar obstacles when implementing RT, responded differently to those obstacles, including one teacher who abandoned RT and others who dramatically altered its recommended implementation. For example, some teachers found that using homogeneous reading groups, which counters typical recommendations for using RT, helped them to reduce the passiveness exhibited by low-achieving students in the heterogeneous groups and to better assess students' progress.

This adaptability and modification encouraged and documented by the researchers is consistent with formative and design experiments, and it illustrates clearly that fidelity, even when it is based on consistent findings from carefully controlled studies, may not always produce uniform and unmitigated success with all students and teachers in all contexts. Hacker and Tenent (2002) clearly documented the broad range of obstacles the teachers encountered, and they documented the diverse ways in which teachers responded to those obstacles. Some teachers followed the traditional RT procedures, whereas others modified RT procedures that had been developed during the study, with one teacher even abandoning RT altogether in favor of other approaches. The researchers explained how and why some teachers modified the instructional intervention and why others teachers made few, if any, changes to the original intervention. They pointed out, for example, that modifications are often needed as teachers take ownership of their learning and construct an understanding of the instructional practice. They also reported how some teachers modified the intervention because students, regardless of their initial reading abilities, lacked the skills needed to benefit from RT. Also, some teachers had difficulty devoting sufficient time to provide scaffolded instruction to small groups, which is often considered to be a vital component of implementing RT, and they thus opted to use RT with the entire class. In summary, Hacker and Tenent's (2002) study, although not characterized by the authors as a formative or design experiment, included many of this approach's defining characteristics, and it illustrates the useful findings produced by this approach and not likely to be easily discovered in other approaches to research.

Yaden and Tam (2000) represent another example in this category. They reported a 6-month case study that was part of a 4-year longitudinal study and that employed ethnographic methods. Their purpose was to examine the effectiveness of an emergent literacy intervention in a private child-care center located in a high-poverty, Spanish-bilingual community. The study was framed by a developmental and constructivist view of emergent literacy as embedded in the sociocultural context of home, community, and school; thus, it was grounded in an explicitly stated theory. The goal of the case study was to understand how the community's and the teacher's funds of knowledge could be incorporated into a preschool literacy program. Although not presented as a formative or design experiment, their data document how modifications were necessary to ensure the effectiveness of the intervention. The researchers devoted 3 months to observing and collecting data on students, teachers, and parents to address the "need to develop a deeper understanding of the social and cultural resources that both the students and teachers bring to the learning contexts in school and how they may impact the planned intervention" (Yaden & Tam, 2000, p. 4). After that period of data collection, they reevaluated the planned intervention so that it would align more closely with the teacher's beliefs and practices, while remaining cognizant of the emergent literacy behaviors that would benefit the children according to the theoretical orientation guiding the study. Specifically, the researchers realized that the teacher's reading style and the shared-reading intervention would be difficult to integrate into instruction based on their initial data collection. However, they also realized that for an intervention to be successfully implemented, they needed to reflect on their own beliefs and biases as researchers, and then work collaboratively with the teacher to develop an intervention that was responsive to the needs of the children and community.

In short, Yaden and Tam's (2000) study included several important characteristics associated with formative and design experiments, even though they described their methodology as a case study. Their investigation was theoretical, goal-oriented, and intervention-centered; it presents a good example of how, through collaboration and iterative cycles, an intervention is modified. Further, it demonstrates that for an intervention to be successful, it is not always the teachers, the children, or the classroom environment that need to be changed, but, at times, the researchers' conceptualization of an intervention. Their reflections about their study reads very much like a rationale for the use of formative and design experiments, even though they were apparently unaware of how their work connected to that approach.

Studies published in practitioner outlets. We located three studies reporting formative experiments in outlets for practitioners. These publications are noteworthy because they suggest the appeal of this approach to practitioners, and they provide examples of how it might inform their work. However, the articles published in these practitioner outlets do not require, and do not allow, adequate space for a detailed elaboration of the research methodology or findings. Thus, they are not included in Figure 3.2. First, Oakley (2003) described a 10-week study aimed at improving the oral reading fluency of 9- and 10-year-old girls as they created an electronic talking book. Second, Massey (2007) presented an 18-month study to improve the comprehension of a second-grade student who participated in tutoring that focused on fluency, work identification, and comprehension. Third, Baumann, Ware, and Edwards (in press) reported a 1-year study that explored the effects of a comprehension vocabulary program on fifth-grade students' word knowledge and appreciation of vocabulary. In this latter study, Ware, the classroom teacher, also was included as a member of the research team and as a coauthor, which clearly demonstrates the collaborative potential of formative and design experiments. Interestingly, all three studies reported both quantitative and qualitative data.

Finally, Calfee, Norman, Trainin, and Wilson (2001), in a chapter in an International Reading Association publication, described a

3-year study to improve the literacy of first-grade students by using a curriculum that introduced the alphabetic system through the articulatory system (e.g., emphasizing manner, place, and voicing to help students attend to the "feel" of sounds). In addition to describing planned and natural variations of the intervention, they identified students who did not make progress during the school year and briefly described a follow-up study with these students.

3.3. How Have Instructional Interventions Been Defined and Implemented?

An instructional intervention is at the center of conducting a formative or design experiment. But what exactly is an instructional intervention? In the examples of studies overviewed previously in this chapter, an intervention has been defined in at least three ways: (1) a single, well-defined instructional activity, usually implemented during a specific time in the schoolday, (2) a change in the physical or organizational environment of the classroom, or (3) a coherent collection of instructional activities aimed at accomplishing a specific instructional goal.

The first definition is most common and most consistent with the origins of this approach to research. That is, the intervention is a single, specific teaching/learning activity, instructional strategy, or type of lesson or lesson framework usually implemented within the time frame allotted for a particular subject area during the schoolday, although the activity may carry over incidentally or strategically to other subject areas. Indeed, Brown's (1992) foundational exploration of design experiments was centered on introducing teaching activities that enabled readers to become more metacognitively active readers. Other literacy studies in Figure 3.2 in which the intervention is defined in this way include Lenski (2001), who studied the directed reading–connecting activity (DR–CA); Palinscar and colleagues (2001), who studied an activity they called guided inquiry supporting multiple literacies (GIsML); and Reinking and Watkins (2000), who studied engaging teachers and students in creating multimedia book reviews.

Neuman's (1999) formative experiment illustrates the second type of intervention. In her study the intervention was "designed to *flood* child-care centers with books and to train staff on effective reading-aloud techniques" (p. 294, emphasis in original).

Figure 3.2. Published formative and design experiments in literacy published in research journals and defining characteristics of this approach (in chronological order)

Study	Theoretical	Goal-Oriented*	Intervention-Centered (time frame)	Adaptive and Iterative	Transformative	Methodologically Diverse
Abbott, Reed, Abbott, & Berninger (1997) *Design experiment*	Model of dynamic assessment to provide effective and efficient instruction in reading and writing	Bring early elementary students to grade level in reading and writing	Tutoring focused on orthographic and phonological awareness, word recognition, fluency, comprehension, writing (1 year)	Duration of components adjusted over time or based on student needs, but no discussion of adaptations	No explicit attention to or evidence of transformation or unanticipated effects	Quantitative: analysis of standardized measures and probes
Jiménez (1997) *Formative experiment*	Theories of comprehension, including decoding/fluency, metacognition, and culturally appropriate literature	*Examine the strategic literacy knowledge and abilities of low-literacy Latino/a middle school students	Students taught to identify unknown vocabulary, integrate prior knowledge, and formulate questions using culturally relevant materials (2 weeks)	No specific adaptations discussed	No explicit attention to or evidence of transformation or unanticipated effects	Qualitative: analysis of classroom observations, student think-alouds, teacher interviews, and researcher's reflexive journal
McLoughlin & Oliver (1998) *Formative experiment*	Sociocultural theory; i.e, learning is socially embedded in culture where there is an interaction between social factors and cognitive development	Change a telelearning environment (distance education) to facilitate higher-order thinking in middle-grade learners	Strategies and language protocols to encourage higher-order thinking; scaffolding through peer discussions, reflective questioning, and problem-based learning (20 weeks)	Data were shared with 5 teachers in different subjects at 3 points and the teachers adapted instruction accordingly	Changes in teacher's pedagogy and use of technology	Qualitative: analysis of teacher talk and student talk

Figure 3.2. (cont'd)

Study	Theoretical	Goal-Oriented*	Intervention-Centered (time frame)	Adaptive and Iterative	Transformative	Methodologically Diverse
Neuman (1999) *Formative experiment*	Frequent and enriching experiences with text fosters children's curiosity about print and provides foundation of literacy	Improve the early literacy abilities of economically disadvantaged preschool children	Child-care staff taught to choose and read high-quality literature to young children in book-sharing activities (8 months)	Training adapted to specific needs of centers, logistical factors, and staff commitment	Changes documented in physical and social environment	Qualitative: analysis of environment and teacher–child interactions Quantitative: analysis of standardized assessments, control sites
Reinking & Watkins (2000) *Formative experiment*	Matthew effects	Increase the amount and diversity of fourth- and fifth-grade students' independent reading	Creating multimedia book reviews as alternative to conventional book report (2 years)	Adaptations based on observational data, teacher input, focus group interviews, etc.	Evidence of transformation (e.g., intervention used in other subjects) and unanticipated findings (e.g., more parental involvement)	Qualitative: field notes, interviews, etc. Quantitative: standardized assessments and control group
Welch (2000) *Formative experiment*	No theory presented	*Understand team teaching and its effectiveness on fourth- and fifth-grade students' learning in reading and/or spelling	Team teaching (16–19 weeks)	No specific adaptations discussed	No explicit attention to or evidence of transformation or unanticipated effects	Qualitative: analysis of focus group interviews, teacher journals, etc. Quantitative: student assessments
De Corte, Verschaffel, & van de Ven (2001) *Design experiment*	Learning environment influences students' adoption and use of comprehension strategies	*Develop, implement, and evaluate research-based strategies for facilitating comprehension in upper-elementary grades	Students taught to use prior knowledge, clarify vocabulary, use schematic representation, identify main idea and meta-cognitive strategies (4 months)	No specific adaptations discussed; explicit aim to maintain fidelity	No explicit attention to or evidence of transformation or unanticipated effects	Qualitative: interviews and observations Quantitative: standardized assessments with control classrooms

Figure 3.2. (cont'd)

Study	Theoretical	Goal-Oriented*	Intervention-Centered (time frame)	Adaptive and Iterative	Transformative	Methodologically Diverse
Duffy (2001) *Formative experiment*	Literacy achievement can be accelerated by balanced instruction, responsive teaching, and quality instruction	Accelerate achievement of struggling second-grade students in summer school	Comprehensive configuration of literacy activities including book talks, read-alouds, discussions, word sorts, making word, etc. (10 weeks)	Instruction adapted to meet the individual needs of each student	No explicit attention to or evidence of transformation or unanticipated effects	Qualitative: analysis of audio/videotapes, classroom, observations, etc. Quantitative: standardized assessments, writing samples, etc.
Lenski (2001) *Formative experiment*	Transactional theory of reading, constructivism, and semiotics	Expand number and variety of third-grade students' intertextual references during discussion	Directed reading-connecting activity (DR–CA) (6 months)	Teacher clarified beliefs and modified intervention to facilitate better discussions	Teacher acquired new beliefs about discussion, valued range of responses; students led more discussions	Qualitative analysis of audio/videotapes and field notes
Palinscar, Magmusson, Collins, & Cutter (2001) *Design experiment*	Inquiry-based instruction	Promote scientific understanding of texts in upper-elementary students with special needs	Guided inquiry supporting multiple literacies (GIsML) (2 years)	Teachers tended to focus on a particular element of the intervention	No explicit attention to or evidence of transformation or unanticipated effects	Qualitative: videotapes, student interviews, etc. Quantitative: student assessments
Saye & Brush (2002) *Generative design experiment*	Problem-based learning well suited to social studies/ history, and critical reasoning about ill-structured domains	Develop a problem-based learning approach for high school social studies teachers grounded in expository tradition	Integrated hypermedia learning environment with a problem-based unit plan (2 years)	Year 2—modifications to the technology, request for teacher to adjust practices	Researchers noted the teacher's shift in pedagogical thinking	Qualitative analysis of group presentations, interviews, observations, and path through a database

Figure 3.2. (cont'd)

Study	Theoretical	Goal-Oriented*	Intervention-Centered (time frame)	Adaptive and Iterative	Transformative	Methodologically Diverse
Porter, DeCusati, & Johnson (2004) *Action research/ design experiment*	Social-ecological theory and research that parent involvement facilitates student achievement	*Investigate the influence of parent classroom volunteers on kindergarteners' early literacy learning	Parent-enriched individual and small-group reading instruction (5 months)	No indication that attempts were made to adapt the intervention	No explicit evidence of efforts to transform the environment beyond intervention	Qualitative: field notes, discussions, etc. Quantitative: parent questionnaire, literacy assessments, etc.
Englert, Zhao, Collings, & Romig (2005) *Design experiment*	No explicit theory, but grounded in research that technology supports literacy development	Evaluate the potential of Internet software to support early reading of first graders at risk for reading difficulties	Use of TELE-Web software (4 weeks in each of two studies)	Study 2 included variations in procedures and modifications to activities	No explicit evidence of efforts to transform the environment beyond intervention	Study 2: Quantitative analysis of activities, student assessment, and observational data
Ivey & Broaddus (2007) *Formative experiment*	Theories of first- and second-language instruction for adolescent English Language Learners	Facilitate, promote engaged reading and writing in a language arts classroom of seventh- and eighth-grade native Spanish speakers	Self-selected readings and teacher-directed reading/writing activities (1 year)	Expanded the range of reading materials, made texts more accessible, etc.	Movement from whole-class to small-group work, etc.	Qualitative: observational notes, artifacts, debriefings, etc. Quantitative: frequency counts of engaged reading, etc.

*Goals marked with an asterisk are goals of the research, not pedagogical goals of the intervention. Studies so marked cannot be considered to represent that defining characteristic of formative and design experiments.

The introduction of many books into classrooms illustrates an intervention that is a planned restructuring of the classroom environment but also implies attending to matters such as how those books are displayed, when and how children have access to them, and so forth.

However, Neuman's (1999) intervention also focused on helping child-care providers (1) understand the importance of literacy in the early years, (2) select books and effectively read aloud to young children, (3) enhance children's responses to stories, and (4) take care of books. Thus, her study also illustrates that the pedagogical goal of a formative or design experiment could focus on changing teachers' attitudes and practices through some type of intervention in the realm of professional development.

A third option is that the intervention consists of a coherent set of activities implemented simultaneously or chosen selectively, perhaps in consultation with a teacher or in response to contextual variables. Duffy's (2001) formative experiment conducted during a 10-week summer remedial class for second-grade struggling readers illustrates the former approach. The instructional intervention consisted of the following set of instructional activities: book talks, read-alouds, discussion, choral reading, word sorts, making words, and writing workshop. The intervention in Ivey and Broaddus's (2007) formative experiment was less specific, initially including two broad categories: (1) self-selected readings and (2) teacher-directed reading and writing activities. Within those broad categories, their investigation was aimed more at discovering the activities that worked rather than testing a specific set of activities. Or, in our own work (Bradley, 2004), the intervention was a collection of activities aimed at increasing the amount and quality of preschool students' verbal interactions, but the activities had different levels of specificity (e.g., book sharing vs. small-group work) and also included restructuring of the environments (environmental changes during mealtimes to allow for more verbal interaction).

These examples illustrate that an intervention may be conceptualized in multiple ways and that each way may suggest methodological variations fitted to the nature of the intervention, how it is implemented, and thus how it might best be studied. However, currently there are no guidelines about matching types of interventions and methodological decisions. That specificity awaits more examples of this approach and more reflection and analysis among the researchers using and critiquing it. However, in general, we believe that the broader and less specific the intervention and the less isolable its use, the more difficult it will be to determine what factors are enhancing or inhibiting its effectiveness and to draw theoretical conclusions. Instructional moves may also be more generic and less specific (e.g., replacing one activity with another as opposed to fine-tuning a lesson). It is also more difficult to determine what aspects of the intervention may account for progress toward the pedagogical goal. Again, these methodological issues need more exploration and reflection among researchers who have a well-developed conceptual and methodological grounding in this approach.

In Figure 3.3, we provide examples of peer-reviewed formative and design experiment studies in areas other than literacy. Although the focus of this book is on literacy research, we recommend examining these studies to understand how researchers in other areas of education are implementing design experiments.

Figure 3.3. Studies published in fields other than literacy that include many of the defining characteristics of formative and design experiments

Study	Topic
Barnett, Harwood, Keating, & Saam (2002) *Design experiment*	To facilitate students' discussion about inquiry-based teaching strategies and to examine teachers' practices and reflections on their pedagogical beliefs
Whipp (2003) *Design experiment*	To study what moves students to higher levels of reflection and inquiry during electronic discussions
Lehrer & Schauble (2004) *Design experiment*	To develop statistical reasoning aimed at increasing fifth-grade students' ability to engage in complex problem solving
Oshima, Oshima, Murayama, Inagaki, Takenaka, Nakayama, & Yamaguchi (2004) *Design experiment*	To transform Japanese elementary science practices into knowledge-building practices
Kawasaki & Herrenkohl (2004) *Design experiment*	To examine the evolution of upper elementary students' theory building and modeling related to a unit on sinking and floating
Wang & Reeves (2006) *Design-based research*	To examine the effects of web-based learning environment about fossilization on the motivation of students in tenth-grade science

CHAPTER 4

Is There a Formative or Design Experiment in Your Future?

We imagine a variety of readers with a variety of purposes reading this book. Some readers may be thinking about conducting a formative or design experiment or collaborating with someone who uses that approach. Others may be interested in critically evaluating a new approach to research that is beginning to appear in the literature. That category might include editors and reviewers of manuscripts reporting a formative or design experiment and faculty who are mentoring doctoral students interested in using this approach. Still others may be considering a more long-term investment in making this approach the mainstay of their research and methodological expertise, including doctoral students ready to launch their careers as literacy researchers.

For readers in that latter category particularly, it would be prudent to consider the viability of formative and design experiments in the long run. Why invest in an approach to research that may fall off the methodological radar in a relatively short period of time? Likewise, some readers may wonder whether the merits of this approach justify selecting it over more conventional experiments or one of the many forms of naturalistic inquiry. Or they may wonder if they have the appropriate perspectives, values, and dispositions to use this approach appropriately and effectively. In this chapter we address such issues and questions.

4.1. What Is the Current Status and Future Potential of this Approach?

In Chapter 1, we traced the diverse disciplinary and methodological roots of formative and design experiments as an emerging approach to education research. Those roots include prominent literacy researchers such as Luis Moll and Ann Brown. Since the appearance of this approach in the late 1980s and early 1990s, interest in formative and design experiments has grown among other literacy researchers. For example, formative experiments have been published in leading peer-reviewed outlets for literacy research such as *Reading Research Quarterly* (e.g., Ivey & Broaddus, 2007; Jiménez, 1997; Neuman, 1999; Reinking & Watkins, 2000). These origins and the highly regarded outlets in which this approach has appeared are a clear indication that this relatively new approach to research has a good pedigree and has been accepted as a legitimate methodological option among mainstream literacy researchers.

Nonetheless, published studies using formative and design experiments represent a decidedly small percentage of the field's published scholarship, and it is an approach to research not widely known or understood among many in the field. Further, the published studies reporting the use of this approach reflect much ambiguity and sometimes distinctly different perspectives about what exactly a formative or design experiment is and about how to plan, conduct, and report one. If there is any conceptual and methodological unity across these studies, it is sometimes little more than a general notion that more flexible research methods and approaches are needed to investigate how interventions related to literacy might be successfully implemented in response to the complexity of authentic educational contexts. These views are often sustained by a sense that conventional research methodologies and their widespread use to investigate instruction in classrooms are inadequate, if not misleading, in producing recommendations useful for practitioners and useful for building meaningful pedagogical theories.

On one hand, we believe that a lack of specificity and clarity is unfortunate and does not bode well for the future of this promising methodology in literacy research. On the other hand, the intuitive appeal of formative and design experiments seems to have tapped a nerve that may allow room for some necessary conceptual and methodological ambiguity and flexibility of interpretations, at least for a while longer. However, the long-term viability of this approach is likely to depend on finding consensus about issues such as its defining characteristics; standards of rigor; and schemes for designing, conducting, and reporting studies. Interestingly, there has been some methodological consistency among literacy researchers. Specifically, three studies published since 2000 (Ivey & Broaddus, 2007; Lenski, 2001; Reinking & Watkins, 2000) have used a common methodological framework, although that framework has not been used among researchers in other fields of education. We hope that this book will contribute to developing more conceptual and methodological specificity about formative and design experiments, particularly among literacy researchers, but also among other education researchers who have conceptualized and used this approach somewhat differently and used different terminology (see van den Akker et al., 2006; Section 1.1.1).

In that regard, trends in education research outside the field of literacy must figure prominently into the current status and future potential of formative and design experiments among literacy researchers. Obviously, if formative and design experiments are adopted more widely among education researchers in general, that methodology in turn is more likely to attract the attention of more literacy researchers. But it is also likely to shape the direction literacy researchers will move in conceptualizing and using formative and design experiments. For example, our review of the literature indicates that education researchers in other areas, particularly educational psychology, math, and science education as well as those interested in digital technologies, have taken the lead in exploring the conceptual and methodological dimensions of formative and design experiments. Evidence of that leadership is found by examining the backgrounds of the contributors to themed issues of *Educational Researcher* (2003, Vol. 32. No. 1), *Educational Psychologist* (2004, Vol. 39, No. 4), and *The Journal of the Learning Sciences* (2004, Vol. 13, No. 1).

Nonetheless, in our estimation, among researchers in other areas of education, there is an imbalance in the literature between efforts to define the conceptual and methodological parameters of this approach and its actual use to conduct empirical studies, although that has been less the case since 2000 (see Figure 3.3). In contrast, literacy researchers have been more likely to plunge into investigations they consider to be formative or design experiments, sometimes with only a rudimentary, and perhaps even erroneous, understanding of the conceptual and methodological foundations of this approach. We hope that this book offsets that tendency in both directions.

We see some evidence that conceptual and methodological clarity is coalescing, especially among researchers in areas outside of literacy (e.g., Gravemeijer & Cobb, 2006, and the other contributors to the volume in which their work appears). However, there appears to be little cross-fertilization between these researchers and literacy researchers who have sometimes conceptualized and implemented this approach differently, with different emphases, and increasingly with different terminology (see Section 1.1.1). For example, virtually no reference is made to the literacy research employing formative and design experiments in a recent edited volume on educational design research (van den Akker et al., 2006). The future of formative and design research, or whatever this approach is eventually called, is not likely to be as bright if researchers interested in this methodology divide themselves into small camps with different conceptual and methodological orthodoxies, especially while this approach still exists on the margins of educational research.

4.1.1. What challenges and obstacles constrain the future of this approach?

Several challenges and obstacles may constrain more widespread use of this approach. A major obstacle is the entrenchment of more established methods and, more importantly, the ingrained aspirations of those who use them. Like most education researchers, literacy researchers want their work to garner the same respect accorded to their colleagues in the hard sciences (in the case of quantitative experimentation) or the social sciences (in the case of qualitative inquiry) (see Lagemann, 2000). Embracing formative and design experiments, to some extent, may mean letting loose of, or at least diluting, those aspirations and aligning one's work with colleagues in engineering rather than in physics or anthropology (see Sloane & Gorard, 2003).

Nonetheless, there are reasons to believe that this is not an insurmountable obstacle. For example, in the late 20th century qualitative researchers broke the hegemony of quantitative methods in education research, and their work is now widely recognized as legitimate and useful. The increased acceptance of mixed methods in education research (e.g., see Johnson & Onwuegbuzie, 2004) may also be beneficial because it introduces an epistemological and methodological perspective distinctly compatible with formative and design experiments. Another positive sign is that, in our experience, many of our colleagues are interested in and open to learning more about formative and design experiments. There is certainly not the acrimony and defensiveness that often accompanied the debates between qualitative and quantitative researchers in the early 1990s.

However, as Schoenfeld (2006) has pointed out, that methodological openness is not currently shared within federal agencies that fund education research. Thus, it is unlikely that there will be substantial funding available to conduct the large-scale, time- and resource-intensive work necessary to identify the critical factors that affect an intervention's effectiveness across contexts, let alone under what conditions it may actually be harmful (see Burkhardt, 2006). On the other hand, currently there is more likelihood of federal funding for formative and design experiments than for naturalistic inquiry, although, in our experience, only when it is couched as an ancillary, less rigorous approach, usually as a prelude to conventional experiments using sophisticated statistical analyses. Like qualitative researchers, those who wish to seek funding for formative and design experiments may need to embed them innocuously in a more dominant frame of scientific experimentation when seeking federal funding, or they may need to turn to private foundations (e.g., the Design-Based Research Collective is funded by the Spencer Foundation).

Another overarching obstacle is the lack of conceptual and methodological clarity about what formative and design experiments really are, how they should be conducted, what standards of rigor are relevant, and how we should view their results, particularly in relation to other methodologies. According to Kelly (2004), to be more than a loose set of methods and to become a full-fledged methodology, this approach must be "under-girded by a conceptual structure that forms the basis for the warrants for [its] claims"; otherwise, it will "contribute only haphazardly to an aggressive science of learning" (p. 118). The variety of terminology used to describe this approach to research (see Section 1.1.1) reflects in part that ambiguity and a lack of conceptual stability. In his critique of design-based research, Dede (2004) characterized it as "a kind of 'Swiss Army Knife' of research . . . [entailing methods that] do a little of everything, but do nothing particularly well" (p.

106). To secure a future in the mainstream of education research, we believe, formative and design experiments will require a clear and consensual articulation of what they do well, why, and how they can be evaluated in relation to agreed-upon standards of rigor. We hope that this book substantively contributes to that goal. Other conceptual and methodological limitations inherent to this approach must also be acknowledged and addressed to secure its future. For example, various critiques have argued that this approach is underconceptualized theoretically because it emphasizes workability (see diSessa & Cobb, 2004) and that it is overmethodologized, producing copious and unwieldy data (e.g., Dede, 2004). Positioning formative and design experiments relative to basic conceptual and methodological issues such as causation and generalization is also an unresolved issue. In the case of causation, for example, Sandoval (2004) argued that "it does not really make sense to try to attribute causality simply to one aspect of the design intervention because the pieces do not operate in isolation from each other" (p. 215). The Design-Based Research Collective (2003), on the other hand, argued that this approach "can generate plausible causal accounts . . . by assisting in the identification of mechanisms [that enrich] our understanding of the intervention itself" (p. 6). In the case of generalization, we believe that convincing arguments can be made that formative and design experiments do produce data and findings that can be generalized, at least if a broader view of generalization is adopted. We discussed that issue in Section 1.4.

There are also more mundane and practical issues that must be addressed. For example, Dede (2004) pointed out that there are no standards or guidelines for "determining when to abandon a design approach as unpromising" or "when an initial implementation is 'good enough' to merit further exploration—or an interesting enough failure" (p. 108). In Chapter 2 we also discussed issues such as whether a researcher's or a teacher's agenda should predominate in a formative or design experiment and how to contend methodologically and interpretively with the common situation in which the researcher plays a dominant role in implementing the intervention being studied.

Other practical issues face researchers interested in conducting and reporting formative or design experiments. For example, how do researchers using this approach seek and gain approval from an Institutional Review Board (IRB) when their research entails a methodology and an intervention that may be constantly changing within a single investigation (see Hemmings, 2006)? How can researchers approach publishing formative and design experiments given the wealth of data this approach tends to produce and the need to ideally accumulate data over extended periods of time across multiple sites? Reeves and colleagues (2005) suggested that researchers adopt the following sequence: Present work at general and discipline-specific conferences, maintain interim findings on a website, occasionally generate syntheses and interim reports and submit them to scholarly journals, and, finally, publish books summarizing the methods, results, and design principles discovered across their work. However, as they point out in regard to peer-reviewed journal publication, many journal editors and reviewers are not familiar with or have misunderstandings about design research.

Another issue that may constrain the advancement of formative and design experiments into the mainstream of research is a lack of programs of study aimed at preparing doctoral students to use this approach to research. Coursework and/or experiences that might be relevant include (1) basic understandings of quantitative, qualitative, and mixed-methods research; (2) collaborative and/or action research, including knowledge of the teacher development literature; (3) critical reviews of the epistemologies of education research, including pragmatism; and, ideally, (4) a course in formative and design experiments or design-based research methods. It is unlikely that qualified faculty would currently be available to teach such a course, except at a few institutions. However, formative and design experiments might for the time being be an interesting topic for faculty and students to explore in an advanced research seminar. We hope this book might be a useful resource toward that end.

4.1.2. What are the key advantages arguing for continued and expanded use?

Despite the obstacles and challenges discussed in the previous section, we remain enthusiastically optimistic about the future of this approach to research. We believe that there is a need for this approach in the methodological landscape, as we discussed in Section 1.1.2, and it has some key conceptual advantages that are intuitively attractive and may lead to wider use.

Foremost, in our view, this approach addresses directly the long-felt need and long-lamented failure among education researchers to align theory, research, and practice to make concrete, meaningful, and readily usable recommendations to practitioners. Prominent literacy researchers have pointed out that our endeavors as a field have been inadequate, if not dysfunctional, in regard to conducting research on interventions in classrooms (e.g., see Dillon et al., 2000; Pressley et al., 2006). Thus, a fundamental advantage of formative and design experiments is that this approach addresses the limitations of conventional methodologies that too often provide practitioners with little more than broad generalizations that have little to do with their day-to-day practice. Put another way, researchers who use conventional research methods position instructional practice as something into which their work must be translated. Researchers who use formative and design experiments, on the other hand, see authentic instructional practice as something that must be accommodated by their research methods and that must also be translated into valid and usable theories.

We believe that this change in emphasis, if not complete reversal, of the normal theory–research–practice sequence that has defined our research is intellectually, intuitively, and emotionally appealing to education researchers. It provides an intermediary ground for research activity that balances a quest for theoretically elegant understandings, rigorously pursued through research, and a desire and obligation to positively transform practice in such a way as to achieve valued pedagogical goals. In that regard, formative and design experiments introduce the powerful and attractive metaphors of engineering and ecology into our discourse about literacy research, how it might be conducted, and toward what ends. We believe that the unleashing of those metaphors within the community of literacy researchers is unlikely to be retracted if this approach to research can continue to be refined conceptually and methodologically, if explicit standards of rigor can be identified, and if there is a steadily improving supply of good examples.

That is, formative and design experiments have the advantage that they provide researchers with a liberating sense of seeking authentic improvement guided by working theories, not just intellectually satisfying abstract theoretical arguments. Further, this approach encourages constructive collaborations among researchers from diverse disciplines and between researchers and teachers. The underlying rationale for formative and design experiments is particularly appealing to teachers, because in one sense it is simply a more systematic approach to the essence of good teaching. That is, teachers have goals for their teaching and at least tacit theories that guide their efforts to achieve them. As they teach, they must adapt their moves to accomplish their goals in light of what does and does not work and sometimes modify the tacit theories that underlie their teaching. Thus, there is a pleasing congruency between the methods of formative and design experiments and the process of teaching, which may be particularly appealing to literacy researchers, many of whom were classroom teachers before they became researchers.

In the same vein, the future of formative and design experiments may be brighter because they represent an approach to research that aligns well with a variety of trends and issues in the field. For example, formative and design experiments are consistent with pragmatic, progressive, and democratic views of education as promoted by Dewey (see Dillon et al., 2000). As such, this approach may be an appealing counterpoint to the excesses of scientism in education research in general and literacy research in particular. At the same time, it avoids the excesses of naturalistic approaches that are decidedly abstract, philosophical, and ideologically complex and that are only marginally attentive to how results may inform practice. We might even imagine that formative and design experiments could one day soon be afforded a higher status among policy makers and funding agencies if this approach can generate convincing recommendations grounded in extensive, rigorous data collection. Finally, as an approach to research that emerged solely within the education research community, it might be imagined to help education research to achieve the status of a full-fledged discipline (see Kuhn, 1970).

4.2. Who Should Consider Conducting a Formative or Design Experiment?

Inspired by the comedian Jeff Foxworthy, and as a way of summarizing some of the dominant themes of formative and design experiments, we respond to this question as follows:

You might be a researcher who uses (or should consider using) formative and design experiments if you . . .

- are interested in investigating how education research might contribute directly to improving teaching and learning.
- are interested in research that takes place in classrooms and involves instructional interventions.
- are interested in testing and developing more specific pedagogical theories grounded in instructional practice instead of overarching theories of teaching and learning.
- do not see a clear distinction between basic and applied research.
- have the inclinations of an engineer who uses theory to accomplish specific ends.
- have a commitment to working closely with practitioners.
- like interdisciplinary, collaborative work.
- see understanding and improving teaching and learning as integrated goals.
- are not particularly attracted to or troubled by debates about ultimate truth.
- have a heightened sense of commitment to democratic values.
- are interested in investigating problems and issues that practitioners identify as important.
- see classrooms as fascinatingly complex ecologies and are comfortable with that complexity.
- are adaptable and flexible methodologically and in your approach to practice.
- are theoretically, philosophically, and methodologically open minded.
- see any research methodology as potentially useful.
- are inclined to consider what is valued pedagogically and why.
- are comfortable using mixed methods.
- are more interested in asking what could be, rather than what is best in general, or simply what is.
- are not committed militantly to a narrow, uncompromising ideological perspective.
- feel comfortable with the tenets of pragmatism as a worldview.

- see scientific inquiry more broadly than controlled experimentation.
- are wary of the concept of best practice or define it circumstantially.
- see theory as having to do work to improve teaching and learning in specific contexts in order to be useful.
- are disappointed in and concerned about the gap between research and practice.

4.3. WHAT DO WE THINK ABOUT FORMATIVE AND DESIGN EXPERIMENTS AFTER WRITING THIS BOOK?

"I write to understand, not to be understood" is an aphorism that captures one reason we wrote this book. That is, writing this book provided a welcome opportunity to delve more deeply into the literature about formative and design experiments and to consolidate, and sometimes to reconcile, the diversity of perspectives associated with this approach from our stance as literacy researchers. It has also allowed us to weigh, and in some instances to temper, our enthusiasm for formative and design experiments in light of a more thorough examination of the literature. Thus, we have come to understand this approach much more deeply than when we started. In this final section we share some insights we have gained and conclusions we have reached.

First, we have a stronger sense of the diverse perspectives contributing to the origins of formative and design experiments. These diverse perspectives continue to mold understandings of an approach to research that is distinctly different from conventional approaches and that has been given many names. Nonetheless, we have found a coherent conceptual core around which those diverse perspectives and conceptualizations revolve. That conceptual core, as we pointed out in the introduction to Chapter 1, reflects an aim to find ways of doing research that coherently align theory, research, and practice in order to achieve valued pedagogical goals; a conviction that conventional methodologies do not adequately serve that aim; and a belief that the only way to proceed is to engage systematically in studying how promising interventions operate in real contexts. The dual metaphors of engineering and ecology capture the essence of that core, as the metaphors of the laboratory and lens capture the essence of conventional approaches to research.

Yet, across the various fields of study in education, there continues to be a diversity of interpretations of that conceptual core and how it is applied methodologically. Different researchers from different backgrounds conceptualize, conduct, and report their work differently; they embed their work in different conceptual and methodological frameworks; and they use different terminology. That diversity may simultaneously represent a strength and a limitation of this approach. Conceptual and methodological flexibility and inclusiveness are desirable characteristics of classroom research and enrich the field (Eisenhart & Borko, 1993). However, flexibility and inclusiveness also inhibit a clear articulation of conceptual and methodological boundaries, precise definitions, and establishment of widely agreed-upon standards of rigor. On the other hand, beyond an agreed-upon conceptual core and general methodological characteristics, seeking a high level of precision about what exactly formative and design experiments or similarly named approaches are may be less of an issue when researchers consider their work to be a pragmatically driven engineering science. Indeed, the press for methodological precision and for precise boundaries between various methodologies and approaches may simply reflect the underlying assumptions and expectations of conventional methodologies driven by a need to mimic the hard or social sciences. In other words, we believe something may be lost if we too quickly or too assuredly try to fence in the way different researchers conceptualize, implement, and report efforts to interpret formative and design experiments, at least beyond the broad parameters we have laid out in this book.

We do not believe that it is necessary for researchers interested in using this methodology to wait for some perfect conceptual and methodological clarity that is currently elusive. In fact, if such clarity is necessary at all, it is only likely to emerge as more researchers boldly explore the fundamental conceptual power of a methodology originating spontaneously among diverse researchers, all of whom sought research methods aimed at understanding how promising interventions could work in real classrooms. New frameworks for conducting formative and design experiments or refinement and validation of existing frameworks as well as a more precise articulation of methodological rigor are likely to be the result of uninhibited methodological exploration without too much concern for seeking methodological orthodoxy. It may very well be that a variety of approaches with a variety of names will eventually emerge and coalesce around a common set of guiding assumptions, but only if researchers are open to new ways to enact the core assumptions and purposes of this new approach.

Indeed, cautious and strategic risk taking is inherent to, or at least compatible with, conducting studies within the methodological perspective we have termed formative and design experiments. For example, each instructional move within a formative or design experiment risks failure. But failure is viewed as useful in this approach because it is an essential component of refining theory and practice (see Sloane & Gorard, 2003; Wagner, 1993). Similarly, as Walker (2006) argued, "Design research that takes greater risks of accepting erroneous conclusions may have higher payoff [than conventional research aimed at overarching theories]. . . . The key to productive design research is to strike a new balance between caution and risk-taking" (p. 11). Thus, a conclusion we draw is that it is time for more researchers to explore more fully the viability of this approach by actually conducting studies grounded in core conceptual understandings (see Chapter 1), a few defining characteristics of this approach (see Section 1.1.2), and basic standards of rigor (see Section 2.3), while using one of several existing frameworks (see Section 2.4) or creating their own framework.

Literacy instruction, we would argue, provides fertile ground for such risk taking, and literacy researchers are in a good position to lead the way. They can draw on a rich base of existing theory and research; an acceptance of diverse research methodologies (see the other volumes in this series); an array of promising interventions often studied previously using conventional methodologies; several prominent examples of formative and design experiments in the literature; and many areas of instruction that are in urgent need of innovative, effective, workable instructional interventions (e.g., strategy instruction, critical reading, digital literacies). In addition, no area of the curriculum has been more politicized in terms of using research to justify, if not dictate, instruction. Thus, formative and design experiments not only represent a potentially rich new source of data and information not produced by other approaches; this approach also raises issues and perspectives that are too often ignored or played down in a search for evidence-based instruction. For example, formative and design experiments raise questions about factors that enhance or inhibit the effectiveness of a generally effective intervention, the conditions under which an intervention may be harmful, and what unanticipated effects might be expected when it is implemented. These are some of the reasons we remain decidedly enthusiastic about this approach's potential contributions to literacy research. We believe it recenters the field on its core mission to inform purposeful efforts to promote literacy development undistracted by more esoteric philosophical and methodological debates. Formative and design experiments and related approaches have significant potential to keep researchers grounded in the reality of day-to-day instructional practice and to generate understandings and recommendations that more directly and authentically inform practitioners. Toward that end, this approach addresses critiques of literacy research that have called for shifting our collective attention toward doing research that is pragmatic (Dillon et al., 2000) and studying interventions in ways that help us understand more precisely how they operate in real practice (Pressly et al., 2006).

We hope that this book will lead other literacy researchers to share our enthusiasm for what we believe to be the strong potential of this approach to bridge the long-standing gap between theory and research and the flexible accommodation to local conditions inherent to successful practice. We hope that it will stimulate more understanding and interest among current researchers, but also especially among those who will become the next generation of researchers, to understand and to accept formative and design experiments into the mainstream of literacy research and perhaps to consider incorporating this approach into their own programs of research. Most of all, we hope that this book becomes part of an ongoing dialogue not only about the advantages, limitations, and viability of formative and design experiments but also about the role of research and research methodology in the field of education in general and literacy education in particular. Conceptually, methodologically, and philosophically, formative and design experiments raise fundamental questions about what we do as literacy researchers and why we do it. Regardless of whether or not this approach enters the mainstream of research, it raises important questions about the past, present, and future goals of education and literacy research and about how we can most effectively go about attaining them. In the end, understanding the underlying rationale and need for formative and design experiments is the essential starting point for planning, doing, and interpreting them.

References

Note: An asterisk denotes a published peer-reviewed study including several of the defining characteristics of formative and design experiments.

*Abbott, S. P., Reed, E., Abbott, R. D., & Beringer, V. W. (1997). Year-long balanced reading/writing tutorial: A design experiment used for dynamic assessment. *Learning Disability Quarterly, 20*(3), 249–263

Arhar, J. M., Holly, M. L., & Kasten, W. C. (2001). *Action research for teachers: Traveling the yellow brick road.* Upper Saddle River, NJ: Merrill Prentice Hall.

Atkin, C. K., & Freimuth, V. (1989). Formative evaluation research in campaign design. In R. E. Rice & C. K. Atkin (Eds.), *Public communication campaigns* (2nd ed.) (pp. 131–136). Newbury Park, CA: Sage.

Baek, J., Kelly, A. E., Cobb, P. A., Lobato, J., Sloane, F. C., Barab, S. A., & Lesh, R. (2006, April). *Developing methodological rigor in design research in education.* Symposium presented at the annual meeting of the American Educational Research Association, Chicago.

Bannan-Ritland, B. (2002). Literacy access online: The development of an online support environment for literacy facilitators working with children with disabilities. *Tech Trends, 45*(2), 17–22.

Bannan-Ritland, B. (2003). The role of design in research: The integrative learning design framework. *Educational Researcher, 32*(1), 21–24.

Barab, S., & Squire, K. (2004). Design-based research: Putting a stake in the ground. *The Journal of the Learning Sciences, 13,* 1–14.

*Barnett, M., Harwood, W., Keating, T., & Saam, J. (2002). Using emerging technologies to help bridge the gap between university theory and classroom practice: Challenges and success. *School Science and Mathematics, 102*(6), 299–313.

Baumann, J. F., Dillon, D. R., Schockley, B. B., Alvermann, D. E., & Reinking, D. (1996). Perspectives in literacy research. In L. Baker, P. P. Afflerbach, & D. Reinking (Eds.), *Developing engaged readers in school and home communities* (pp. 217–245). Mahwah, NJ: Erlbaum.

*Baumann, J. F., Ware, D., & Edwards, E. C. (in press). "Bumping into spicy, tasty words that catch your tongue": A formative experiment on vocabulary instruction. *The Reading Teacher.*

Beach, R. (2000). Reading and responding to literature at the level of activity. *Journal of Literacy Research, 32*(2), 237–251.

Bell, P. (2004). On the theoretical breadth of design-based research in education. *Educational Psychologist, 39,* 243–253.

Bradley, B. A. (2004) A formative experiment to enhance verbal interactions in a preschool classroom. Unpublished doctoral dissertation, University of Georgia, Athens.

Brown, A. L. (1992). Design experiments: Theoretical and methodological challenges in creating complex interventions in classroom settings. *The Journal of the Learning Sciences, 2*(2), 141–178.

Brown, A. L., & Campione, J. C. (1996). Psychological theory and the design of innovative learning environments: On procedures, principles, and systems. In R. Glaser (Ed.), *Innovations in learning: New environments for education* (pp. 289–325). Mahwah, NJ: Erlbaum.

Bruce, B. C., & Rubin, A. (1993). *Electronic quills: A situated evaluation of using computers for classroom writing.* Hillsdale, NJ: Erlbaum.

Burkhardt, H. (2006). From design research to large-scale impact: Engineering research in education. In J. van den Akker, K. Gravemeijer, S. McKenney, & N. Nieveen (Eds.), *Educational design research* (pp. 121–150). New York: Routledge.

Burnaford, G., Fischer, J., & Hobson, D. (Eds.) (2001). *Teachers doing research: The power of action through inquiry* (2nd ed.). Mahwah, NJ: Erlbaum.

Calfee, R. C., Norman, K. A., Trainin, G., & Wilson, K. M. (2001). Conducting a design experiment for improving early literacy: What we learned in school last year. In C. M. Roller (Ed.), *Learning to teach reading: Setting the research agenda.* Newark, DE: International Reading Association.

Chatterji, M. (2004). Evidence on "what works": An argument of extended-term mixed-method (ERMM) evaluation designs. *Educational Researcher, 33*(9), 3–13.

Cherryholmes, C. H. (1992). Notes on pragmatism and scientific realism. *Educational Researcher, 21*(6), 13–19.

Cobb, P., Confrey, J., diSessa, A., Lehrer, R., & Schauble, L. (2003a). Design experiments in educational research. *Educational Researcher, 32*(1), 9–13.

Cobb, P., McClain, K., & Gravemeijer, K. (2003b). Learning about statistical covariation. *Cognition and Instruction, 21,* 1–78.

Cochran-Smith, M., & Lytle, S.L. (1999). Relationships of knowledge and practice: Teaching learning in communities. In A. Iran-Nejad & P. D. Pearson (Eds.), *Review of Research in Education* (vol. 24) (pp. 249–306). Washington, DC: American Educational Research Association.

Cole, A. L., & Knowles, J. G. (1993). Teacher development partnership research: A focus on methods and issues. *American Educational Research Journal, 30*(3), 473–495.

Collins, A. (1992). Toward a design science of education. In E. Scanlon & T. O'Shea (Eds.), *New directions in educational technology.* New York: Springer-Verlag.

Collins, A. (1999). The changing infrastructure of education research. In E. C. Lagemann & L. B. Shulman (Eds.), *Issues in educational research: Problems and possibilities* (pp. 289–298). San Francisco: Jossey-Bass.

Creswell, J. W. (2002). *Educational research: Planning, conducting, and evaluating quantitative and qualitative research.* Upper Saddle River, NJ: Merrill Prentice Hall.

Cronbach, L. S. (1975). Beyond the two disciplines of scientific psychology. *American Psychologist, 30,* 116–127.

*De Corte, E., Verschaffel, L., & van de Ven, A. (2001). Improving text comprehension strategies in upper primary school children: A design experiment. *British Journal of Educational Psychology, 71,* 531–559.

Dede, C. (2004). If design-based research is the answer, what is the question? A commentary on Collins, Joseph, and Bielaczyc; diSessa and Cobb; and Fishman, Marx, Bleumenthal, Krajcik, and Soloway in the *JLS* special issue on design-based research. *The Journal of the Learning Sciences, 13,* 105–114.

Design-Based Research Collective, The. (2003). Design-based research: An emerging paradigm for educational inquiry. *Educational Researcher, 32*(1), 5–8.

Diaz, S., Moll, L. C., & Mehan, H. (1986). Sociocultural resources in instruction: A context-specific approach. In C. E. Cortes & California Office of Bilingual Education (Ed.), *Beyond Language: Social and Cultural Factors in Schooling Language Minority Students* (pp. 299–343). Los Angeles: California State University, Evaluation, Dissemination, and Assessment Center (ERIC Document Reproduction Services, No. ED 304 241).

Dickinson, D. K., & Tabors, P. O. (2001). *Beginning literacy with language.* Baltimore: Paul H. Brookes.

Dillon, D. R., O'Brien, D. G., & Heilman, E. E. (2000). Literacy research in the next millennium: From paradigms to pragmatism and practicality. *Reading Research Quarterly, 35,* 10–26.

diSessa, A. A., & Cobb, P. (2004). On ontological innovation and the role of theory in design experiments. *The Journal of the Learning Sciences, 13*(1), 77–103.

*Duffy, A. M. (2001). Balanced, literacy acceleration, and responsive teaching in a summer school literacy program for elementary school struggling readers. *Reading Research and Instruction, 40*(2), 67–100.

Duffy, G. G. (1994). How teachers think of themselves: A key to mindfulness. In J. N. Mangieri & C. Collins (Eds.), *Creating powerful thinking in teachers and students: Diverse perspectives* (pp. 3–25). Fort Worth, TX: HarperCollins.

Ebel, R. (1982). The future of educational research. *Educational Researcher, 22*(7), 18–19.

Eisenhart, M., & Borko, H. (1993). *Designing classroom research: Themes, issues, and struggles.* Boston: Allyn & Bacon.

Engeström, Y., Miettinen, R., & Punamäki, R.-L. (Eds.). (1998). *Perspectives on activity theory.* Cambridge, UK: Cambridge University Press.

*Englert, C. S., Zhao, Y., Collings, N., & Romig, N. (2005). Learning to read words: The effects of internet-based software on the improvement of reading performance. *Remedial and Special Education, 26*(6), 357–370.

Firestone, W. A. (1993). Alternative arguments for generalizing from data as applied to qualitative research. *Educational Researcher, 22*(4), 16–23.

Garfield, V. (2000). *A formative experiment investigating the use of electronic portfolios as a means of improving elementary students' perceptions of themselves as readers.* Unpublished doctoral dissertation, University of Georgia, Athens.

Gersten, R. (2005). Behind the scenes of an intervention research study. *Learning Disabilities Research and Practice, 20*(4), 200–212.

Gersten, R., Baker, S. K., Smith-Johnson, J., Dimino, J., & Peterson, A. (2006). Eyes of the prize: Teaching complex historical content to middle school students with learning disabilities. *Exceptional Children, 72*(3), 264–280.

Gravemeijer, K., & Cobb, P. (2006). Design research from a learning design perspective. In J. van den Akker, K. Gravemeijer, S. McKenney & N. Nieveen (Eds.), *Educational design research* (pp. 17–51). New York: Routledge.

Guba, E. G., & Lincoln, Y. S. (1994). Competing paradigms in qualitative research. In N. K. Denzin & Y. S. Lincoln (Eds.), *Handbook of qualitative research* (pp. 105–117). Thousand Oaks, CA: Sage.

*Hacker, D., & Tenent, A. (2002). Implementing reciprocal teaching in the classroom: Overcoming obstacles and making modifications. *Journal of Educational Psychology, 94*(4), 699–718.

Harste, J. C. (1993). Response to Ridgeway, Dunston, & Qian: Standards for instructional research. *Reading Research Quarterly, 28*(4), 356–358.

Hemmings, A. (2006). Great ethical divides: Bridging the gap between Institutional Review Boards and researchers. *Educational Researcher, 35*(2), 12–18.

Hoadley, C. M. (2004). Methodological alignment in design-based research. *Educational Psychologist, 39,* 203–212.

Howe, K. R. (1988). Against the quantitative–qualitative incompatibility thesis or dogmas die hard. *Educational Researcher, 17,* 10–16.

Hostetler, K. (2005). What is "good" education research? *Educational Researcher 34*(6), 16–21.

*Ivey, G., & Broaddus, K. (2007). A formative experiment investigating literacy engagement among adolescent Latina/o students beginning to read, write, and speak English. *Reading Research Quarterly, 42,* 512–545.

Jacob, E. (1992). Culture, context, and cognition. In M. D. Lecompte, W. L. Millroy, & J. Preissle (Eds.), *The handbook of qualitative research in education* (pp. 293–335). San Diego, CA: Academic Press.

*Jiménez, R. T. (1997). The strategic reading abilities and potential of five low-literacy Latina/o readers in middle school. *Reading Research Quarterly, 32,* 224–243.

Johnson, R. B., & Onwuegbuzie, A. J. (2004). Mixed methods research: A research paradigm whose time has come. *Educational Researcher, 33*(7), 14–36.

Joseph, D. (2004). The practice of design-based research: Uncovering the interplay between design, research, and the real-world context. *Educational Psychologist, 39*(4), 235–242.

Kamberelis, G., & de la Luna, L. (1998). Walking the walk without talking the talk: Researching (un)common ground in collaborative action research in literacy classrooms. In T. Shanahan & F. V. Rodriguez-Brown (Eds.), *Forty-seventh Yearbook of the National Reading Conference* (pp. 472–484). Chicago: National Reading Conference.

Kamberelis, G., & Dimitriadis, G. (2004). *On qualitative inquiry.* New York: Teachers College Press.

*Kawasaki, K., & Herrenkohl, L. R. (2004). Theory building and modeling in a sinking and floating unit: A case study of third and fourth grade students' developing epistemologies of science. *International Journal of Science Education, 17*(11), 1299–1324.

Kelly, A. E. (2004). Design research in education: Yes, but is it methodological? *The Journal of the Learning Sciences, 13,* 115–128.

Kelly, A. E., & Lesh, R. A. (Eds.). (2000). *Handbook of research design in mathematics and science education.* Mahwah, NJ: Erlbaum.

Kuhn, T. (1970). *The structure of scientific revolutions.* (2nd ed.). Chicago: University of Chicago Press.

Labaree, D. (1998). Educational researchers: Living with a lesser form of knowledge. *Educational Researcher, 27*(8), 4–12.

Lagemann, E. C. (2000). *An elusive science: The troubling history of education research.* Chicago: University of Chicago Press.

*Lehrer, R., & Schauble, L. (2004). Modeling natural variation through distribution. *American Educational Research Journal, 41,* 635–679.

*Lenski, S. D. (2001). Intertextual connections during discussions about literature. *Reading Psychology, 22,* 313–335.

Leu, D., & Reinking, D. (2006, May). *A federally funded project to develop and successfully implement internet-based reading comprehension: An overview.* Paper presented at the annual meeting of the International Reading Association, Chicago.

Levin, M., & Greenwood, D. (2001). Pragmatic action research and the struggle to transform universities into learning communities. In P. Reason & H. Bradbury (Eds.), *Handbook of action research: Participative inquiry and practice* (pp. 103–113). London: Sage.

Lewis, C., Perry, R., & Murata, A. (2006). How should research contribute to instructional improvement? The case of lesson study. *Educational Researcher, 35*(3), 3–14.

*Massey, D. D. (2007). "The Discovery Channel said so" and other barriers to comprehension. *The Reading Teacher, 60*(7), 656–666.

Maxey, S. J. (2003). Pragmatic threads in mixed methods research in the social sciences: The search for multiple modes of inquiry and the end of the philosophy of formalism. In A. Tashakkori & C. Teddlie (Eds.), *Handbook of mixed methods in social and behavioral research* (pp. 51–89). Thousand Oaks, CA: Sage.

McCandliss, B. D., Kalchman, M., & Bryant, P. (2003). Design experiments and laboratory approaches to learning: Steps toward collaborative exchange. *Educational Researcher, 32*(1), 14–16.

McKenney, S., van den Akker, J. J., Burkhardt, H., Cobb, P. A., Edelson, D. C., Gravemeijer, K. P., Kelly, A. E., Phillips, D. C., Reeves, T. C., & Sloane, F. C. (2006, April). *Design research: Principled improvement of learning and instruction.* Symposium presented at the annual meeting of the American Educational Research Association, Chicago.

*McLaughlin, C., & Oliver, R. (1998). Planning a telelearning environment to foster higher-order thinking. *Distance Education, 19*(2), 242–264.

Messick, S. (1992). The interplay of evidence and consequences in the validation of performance assessments. *Educational Researcher, 23*(2), 13–23.

Moll, L., & Diaz, S. (1987). Change as the goal of educational research. *Anthropology & Education Quarterly, 18,* 300–311.

National Reading Panel. (2000). *Teaching children to read: An evidence-based assessment of the scientific research literature on reading and its implications for reading instruction.* Washington, DC: National Institutes of Health, National Institute of Child Health and Human Development.

*Neuman, S. B. (1999). Books make a difference: A study of access to literacy. *Reading Research Quarterly, 34,* 286–311.

Newman, D. (1990). Opportunities for research on the organizational impact of school computers. *Educational Researcher, 19,* 8–13.

Newman, D. (1992). Formative experiments on the co-evolution of technology and the educational environment. In E. Scanlon & T. O'Shea (Eds.), *New directions in educational technology* (pp. 61–70).

Newman, D., Griffin, P., & Cole, M. (1989). *The construction zone: Working for cognitive change in school.* Cambridge, UK: Cambridge University Press.

*Oakley, G. (2003). Improving oral reading fluency (and comprehension) through the creation of talking books. *Reading Online, 6*(7). Retrieved July 26, 2007 from: http://www.readingonline.org/articles/art_index.asp?HREF=oakley/index.html

*Oshima, J., Oshima, R., Murayama, I., Inagaki, S., Takenaka, M., Nakayama, H., & Yamaguchi, E. (2004). Design experiments in Japanese elementary science education with computer support for collaborative learning: Hypothesis testing and collaborative construction. *International Journal of Science Education, 26*(10), 1199–1221.

Otto, W. (1992). The role of reading research in instruction. In S. J. Samuels & A. E. Farstrup (Eds.), *What research has to say about reading instruction* (pp. 1–16). Newark, DE: International Reading Association.

*Palinscar, A. S., Magnusson, S. J., Collins, K. M., & Cutter, J. (2001). Making science accessible to all: Results of a design experiment in inclusive classrooms. *Learning Disabilities Quarterly, 24*(1), 15–32.

Phillips, D. C. (2006). Assessing the quality of design research proposals. In J. van den Akker, K. Gravemeijer, S. McKenney, & N. Nieveen (Eds.), *Educational design research* (pp. 93–99). New York: Routledge.

Pogrow, S. (1996). Reforming the wannabe reformers: Why education reforms almost always end up making things worse. *Phi Delta Kappan, 77,* 656–663.

*Porter DeCusati, C. L., & Johnson, J. E. (2004). Parents as classroom volunteers and kindergarten students' emergent reading skills. *Journal of Educational Psychology, 97*(5), 235–246.

Pressley, M., Graham, S., & Harris, K. (2006). The state of educational intervention research as viewed through the lens of literacy intervention. *British Journal of Educational Psychology, 76,* 1–19.

Purcell-Gates, V. (2004). Ethnographic research. In N. K. Duke & M. H. Mallette (Eds.), *Literacy research methods* (pp. 92–111). New York: Guilford.

Purcell-Gates, V. (2006, December). *What's it all about? Literacy research and civil responsibility.* Presidential address for the National Reading Conference, Los Angeles, CA.

Reason, P., & Bradbury, H. (2001). Introduction: Inquiry and participation in search of a world worthy of human aspiration. In P. Reason & H. Bradbury (Eds.), *Handbook of action research: Participative inquiry and practice* (pp. 1–14). London: Sage.

Reeves, T. (2006). Design research from a technology perspective. In J. van den Akker, K. Gravemeijer, S. McKenney, & N. Nieveen (Eds.), *Educational design research* (pp. 52–66). New York: Routledge.

Reeves, T., Herrington, J., & Oliver, R. (2005). Design research: A socially responsible approach to instructional technology research in higher education. *Journal of Computing in Higher Education, 16,* 97–116.

Reigeluth, C. M. (1999). What is instructional-design theory and how is it changing? In C. M. Reigeluth (Ed.), *Instructional-design theories and models: Volume II. A new paradigm of instructional theory* (pp. 5–29). Mahwah, NJ: Erlbaum.

Reigeluth, C. M., & Frick, T. W. (1999). Formative research: A methodology for creating and improving design theories. In C. M. Reigeluth (Ed.), *Instructional-design theories and models: Volume II: A new paradigm of instructional theory* (pp. 633–651). Mahwah, NJ: Erlbaum.

Reinking, D. (2007). Toward a good or better understanding of best practice. *Journal of Curriculum and Instruction, 1*(1), 75–88.

Reinking, D., & Alvermann, D. E. (2005). What are evaluation studies, and should they be published in RRQ? *Reading Research Quarterly, 40*(2), 142–146.

Reinking, D., & Bradley, B. A. (2004). Connecting research and practice using formative and design experiments. In N. K. Duke & M. H. Mallette (Eds.), *Literacy research methodologies* (pp. 149–169). New York: Guilford.

Reinking, D., & Pickle, M. (1993). Using a formative experiment to study how computers affect reading and writing in classrooms. In D. J. Leu & C. K. Kinzer (Eds.), *Examining central issues in literacy research, theory, and practice* (pp. 263–270). Chicago: National Reading Conference.

Reinking, D., & Watkins, J. (1998). Balancing change and understanding in literacy research through formative experiments. In T. Shanahan & F. Rodriguez-Brown (Eds.), *Forty-Seventh Yearbook of the National Reading Conference* (pp. 461–471). Chicago: National Reading Conference.

*Reinking, D., & Watkins, J. (2000). A formative experiment investigating the use of multimedia book reviews to increase elementary students independent reading. *Reading Research Quarterly, 35*(3), 384–419.

Robson, C. (2002). *Real world research: A resource for social scientists and practitioner-researchers* (2nd ed.). Maldin, MA: Blackwell.

Rorty, R. (1991). *Objectivity, relativism, and truth: Philosophical papers* (Vol. 1). Cambridge, UK: Cambridge University Press.

Salomon, G. (1991). Transcending the qualitative-quantitative debate: The analytic and systemic approaches to educational research. *Educational Researcher, 20*(6), 10–18.

Sandoval, W. A. (2004). Developing learning theory by refining conjectures embodied in educational designs. *Educational Psychologist, 39*(4), 213–223.

*Saye, J. W., & Brush, T. (2002). Scaffolding critical reasoning about history and social issues in multimedia-supported learning environments. *Educational Technology Research and Development, 50*(3), 77–96.

Schoenfeld, A. H. (2006). Design experiments. In J. L. Green, G. Camilli, P. B. Elmore, A. Skukauskaite, & E. Grace (Eds.), *Handbook of complementary methods in education research* (pp. 193–205). Mahwah, NJ: Erlbaum.

Schön, D. A. (1987). *Educating the reflective practitioner.* San Francisco: Jossey-Bass.

Shavelson, R. J., Phillips, D. C., Towne, L., & Feur, M. J. (2003). On the science of education design studies. *Educational Researcher, 32*(1), 25–28.

Sloane, F. C., & Gorard, S. (2003). Exploring modeling aspects of design experiments. *Educational Researcher, 32*(1), 29–31.

Smagorinsky, P., & Jordahl, A. (1991). The student teacher/cooperating teacher collaborative study: A new source of knowledge. *English Education, 23*(1), 54–59.

Snow, C. E., Burns, M. S., & Griffin, P. (Eds.). (1998). *Preventing reading difficulties in young children.* Washington, DC: National Academy Press.

Snyder, I. (1992). "It's not as simple as you think!" Collaboration between a research and a teacher. *English Teacher, 24*(4), 195–211.

Stanovich, K. E. (1986). Matthew effects in reading: Some consequences of individual differences in the acquisition of literacy. *Reading Research Quarterly, 21,* 360–407.

Stanovich, K. E. (2000). *Progress in understanding reading: Scientific foundations and new frontiers.* New York: Guilford.

Stokes, D. E. (1997). *Pasteur's quadrant: Basic science and technological innovation.*. Washington, DC: Brookings Institution Press.

Storch, S. A., & Whitehurst, G. J. (2002). Oral language and code-related precursors to reading: Evidence from a longitudinal structural model. *Developmental Psychology, 38*(6), 934–947.

Strauss, A., & Corbin, J. (1990). *Basics of qualitative research.* Newbury Park, CA: Sage.

Tabak, I. (2004). Reconstructing context: Negotiating the tension between exogenous and endogenous educational design. *Educational Psychologist, 39,* 225–233.

Tafel, L. S., & Fischer, J. C. (2001). Teacher action research and professional development: Foundations for educational renewal. In G. Burnaford, J. Fischer, & D. Hobson (Eds.), *Teachers doing research: The power of action through inquiry* (pp. 221–236). Mahwah, NJ: Erlbaum.

Tashakkori, A., & Teddlie, C. (1998). *Mixed methodology: Combining qualitative and quantitative approaches.* Thousand Oaks, CA: Sage.

Tashakkori, A., & Teddlie, C. (Eds.) (2003). *Handbook of mixed methods in social and behavioral research.* Thousand Oaks, CA: Sage.

van den Akker, J. (1999). Principles and methods of development research. In J. van den Akker, N. Nieveen, R. M. Branch, K. L. Gustafson, & T. Plomp (Eds.), *Design approaches and tools in education and training* (pp. 1–14). Dordrecht, NL: Kluwer Academic Publishers.

van den Akker, J. J., Burkhardt, H., Cobb, P. A., Edelson, D. C., Gravemeijer, K. P., Kelly, A. K., Phillips, D. C., Reeves, T. C., & Sloane, F. C. (2006, April). *Design research: Principled improvement of learning and instruction.* Paper presented at the annual meeting of the American Educational Research Association, San Francisco.

van den Akker, J., Gravemeijer, K. P., McKenney, S, & Nieveen, N. (Eds.) (2006). *Educational design research.* London, UK: Routledge.

Wagner, J. (1993). Ignorance in educational research: Or how can you *not* know that? *Educational Researcher, 22*(5), 15–23.

Walker, D. (2006). Toward productive design studies. In J. van den Akker, K. Gravemeijer, S. Mckenney, & N. Nieveen (Eds.), *Educational design research* (pp. 8–13). New York: Routledge.

*Wang, S., & Reeves, T. C. (2006). The effects of a web-based learning environment on student motivation in a high school earth science course. *Educational Technology, Research and Development, 54*(6), 597–621.

*Welch, M. (2000). Descriptive analysis of team teaching in two elementary classrooms: A formative experimental approach. *Remedial and Special Education, 24,* 366–376.

*Whipp, J. L. (2003). Scaffolding critical reflection in online discussions: Helping prospective teachers think deeply about field experiences in urban schools. *Journal of Teacher Education, 54*(4), 321–333.

Wilson, S .M., & Berne, J. (1999). Teacher learning and the acquisition of professional knowledge: An examination of research on contemporary professional development. In A. Iran-Nejad & P. D. Pearson (Eds.), *Review of Research in Education* (Vol. 24) (pp. 173–209). Washington, DC: American Educational Research Association.

*Yaden, D. B., & Tam, A. (2000). Enhancing emergent literacy in a preschool program through teacher-research collaboration (Report No. 2–001). Center for the Improvement of Early Reading Achievement, University of Michigan.

Index

SUBJECT INDEX

Note: The abbreviation F&DE is used in place of the term "formative and design experiments."

About the Authors

David Reinking is the Eugene T. Moore Professor of Teacher Education at Clemson University. He has served as editor of the *Journal of Literacy Research* (1995–2001) and co-editor of *Reading Research Quarterly* (2001–2007). His scholarly work focuses on the relation between digital technologies and literacy. That work has been published in the field's major outlets such as *Reading Research Quarterly, The Reading Teacher,* and the *Handbook of Reading Research, Volume II.* He also served as lead editor of the first volume of the *Handbook of Literacy and Technology,* which won the Edward B. Fry book award from the National Reading Conference and was cited as one of the best academic books of the year by the American Library Association. Since the mid-1990s, he has written extensively about formative and design experiments and has used that approach in his research. That research has been supported by federal grants from the Office of Educational Research and Improvement and the Institute of Education Sciences in the United States Department of Education. In 2007 he was elected to become President of the National Reading Conference in 2009.

Barbara A. Bradley is an assistant professor in the Department of Curriculum and Teaching at the University of Kansas. She teaches courses on emergent literacy and reading instruction. Her research interests include early literacy, teacher–child language interactions, and book sharing. To pursue those interests, she has conducted formative experiments. Her work has been supported by federally funded grants related to reading fluency, professional development for early childhood teachers, and early literacy for preschool-aged children.